YOUR PERSONAL

ASTROLOGY

PLANNER

TAURUS
2009

YOUR PERSONAL
ASTROLOGY
PLANNER

TAURUS
2009

RICK LEVINE **& JEFF** JAWER

STERLING

New York / London
www.sterlingpublishing.com

2 4 6 8 10 9 7 5 3 1

Published by Sterling Publishing Co., Inc.
387 Park Avenue South, New York, NY 10016
© 2008 by Sterling Publishing Co., Inc.
Text © 2008 Rick Levine and Jeff Jawer
Distributed in Canada by Sterling Publishing
c/o Canadian Manda Group, 165 Dufferin Street
Toronto, Ontario, Canada M6K 3H6
Distributed in the United Kingdom by GMC Distribution Services
Castle Place, 166 High Street, Lewes, East Sussex, England BN7 1XU
Distributed in Australia by Capricorn Link (Australia) Pty. Ltd.
P.O. Box 704, Windsor, NSW 2756, Australia

Sterling ISBN: 978-1-4027-5034-2

For information about custom editions, special sales, premium and
corporate purchases, please contact Sterling Special Sales
Department at 800-805-5489 or
specialsales@sterlingpublishing.com.

TABLE OF CONTENTS

THE PURPOSE OF THIS BOOK

The more you learn about yourself, the better able you are to wisely use the energies in your life. For more than 3,000 years, astrology has been the sharpest tool in the box for describing the human condition. Used by virtually every culture on the planet, astrology continues to serve as a link between individual lives and planetary cycles. We gain valuable insights into personal issues with a birth chart, and can plot the patterns of the year ahead in meaningful ways for individuals as well as groups. You share your sun sign with eight percent of humanity. Clearly, you're not all going to have the same day, even if the basic astrological cycles are the same. Your individual circumstances, the specific factors of your entire birth chart, and your own free will help you write your unique story.

The purpose of this book is to describe the energies of the Sun, Moon, and planets for the year ahead and help you create your future, rather than being a victim of it. We aim to facilitate your journey by showing you the turns ahead in the road of life and hopefully the best ways to navigate them.

YOU ARE THE STAR
OF YOUR LIFE

It is not our goal to simply predict events. Rather, we are reporting the planetary energies—the cosmic weather in which you are living—so that you understand these conditions and know how to use them most effectively.

The power, though, isn't in the stars, but in your mind, your heart, and the choices that you make every day. Regardless of how strongly you are buffeted by the winds of change or bored by stagnation, you have many ways to view any situation. Learning about the energies of the Sun, Moon, and planets will both sharpen and widen your perspective, thereby giving you additional choices.

The language of astrology is a gift of awareness, not a rigid set of rules. It works best when blended with common sense, intuition, and self-trust. This is your life, and no one knows how to live it as well as you. Take what you need from this book and leave the rest. Although the planets set the stage for the year ahead, you're the writer, director, and star of your life and you can play the part in whatever way you choose. *Your Personal Astrology Planner* uses information about your sun sign to give you a better understanding of how the planetary waves will wash upon your shore. We each navigate our lives through time, and each moment has unique qualities. Astrology gives us the ability to describe the constantly changing timescape. For example, if you know the trajectory and the speed of an approaching storm, you can choose to delay a leisurely afternoon sail on the bay, thus avoiding an unpleasant situation.

By reading this book, you can improve your ability to align with the cosmic weather, the larger patterns that affect you day to day. You can become more effective by aligning with the cosmos and cocreating the year ahead with a better understanding of the energies around you.

Astrology doesn't provide quick fixes to life's complex issues. It doesn't offer neatly packed black-and-white answers in a world filled with an infinite variety of shapes and colors. It can, however, give you a much clearer picture of the invisible forces influencing your life.

ENERGY & EVENTS

Two sailboats can face the same gale yet travel in opposite directions as a result of how the sails are positioned. Similarly, how you respond to the energy of a particular set of circumstances may be more responsible for your fate than the given situation itself. We delineate the energetic winds for your year ahead, but your attitude shapes the unfolding events, and your responses alter your destiny.

This book emphasizes the positive, not because all is good, but because astrology shows us ways to transform even the power of a storm into beneficial results. Empowerment comes from learning to see the invisible energy patterns that impact the visible landscape as you fill in the details of your story every day on this spinning planet, orbited by the Moon, lit by the Sun, and colored by the nuances of the planets.

You are a unique point in an infinite galaxy of unlimited possibilities, and the choices that you make have consequences. So use this book in a most magical way to consciously improve your life.

MOON CHARTS

2009 NEW MOONS

Each New Moon marks the beginning of a cycle. In general, this is the best time to plant seeds for future growth. Use the days preceeding the New Moon to finish old business prior to starting what comes next. The focused mind can be quite sharp during this phase. Harness the potential of the New Moon by stating your intentions—out loud or in writing—for the weeks ahead. Hold these goals in your mind; help them grow to fruition through conscious actions as the Moon gains light during the following two weeks. In the chart below, the dates and times refer to when the Moon and Sun align in each zodiac sign (see p16), initiating a new lunar cycle.

DATE	TIME	SIGN
January 26	2:55 AM EST	Aquarius (ECLIPSE)
February 24	8:35 PM EST	Pisces
March 26	12:06 PM EDT	Aries
April 24	11:23 PM EDT	Taurus
May 24	8:11 AM EDT	Gemini
June 22	3:35 PM EDT	Cancer
July 21	10:35 PM EDT	Cancer (ECLIPSE)
August 20	6:02 AM EDT	Leo
September 18	2:44 PM EDT	Virgo
October 18	1:33 AM EDT	Libra
November 16	2:14 PM EST	Scorpio
December 16	7:02 AM EST	Sagittarius

2009 FULL MOONS

The Full Moon reflects the light of the Sun as subjective feelings reflect the objective events of the day. Dreams seem bigger; moods feel stronger. The emotional waters run with deeper currents. This is the phase of culmination, a turning point in the energetic cycle. Now it's time to listen to the inner voices. Rather than starting new projects, the two weeks after the Full Moon are when we complete what we can and slow our outward expressions in anticipation of the next New Moon. In this chart, the dates and times refer to when the moon is opposite the sun in each zodiac sign, marking the emotional peak of each lunar cycle.

DATE	TIME	SIGN
January 10	10:27 PM EST	Cancer
February 9	9:49 AM EST	Leo **(ECLIPSE)**
March 10	10:38 PM EDT	Virgo
April 9	10:56 AM EDT	Libra
May 9	12:01 AM EDT	Scorpio
June 7	2:12 PM EDT	Sagittarius
July 7	5:21 AM EDT	Capricorn **(ECLIPSE)**
August 5	8:55 PM EDT	Aquarius **(ECLIPSE)**
September 4	12:03 PM EDT	Pisces
October 4	2:10 AM EDT	Aries
November 2	2:14 PM EST	Taurus
December 2	2:30 AM EST	Gemini
December 31	2:12 PM EST	Cancer **(ECLIPSE)**

ASTROLOGY, YOU & THE WORLD

WELCOME TO YOUR SUN SIGN

The Sun, Moon, and Earth and all the planets lie within a plane called the **ecliptic** and move through a narrow band of stars made up by 12 constellations called the **zodiac**. The Earth revolves around the Sun once a year, but from our point of view, it appears that the Sun moves through each sign of the zodiac for one month. There are 12 months and astrologically there are 12 signs. The astrological months, however, do not match our calendar, and start between the 19th and 23rd of each month. Everyone is born to an astrological month, like being born in a room with a particular perspective of the world. Knowing your sun sign provides useful information about your personality and your future, but for a more detailed astrological analysis, a full birth chart calculation based on your precise date, time, and place of birth is necessary. Get your complete birth chart online at:

http://www.tarot.com/astrology/astroprofile

This book is about your zodiac sign. Your Sun is in the earth sign of solid Taurus, the determined Bull. Your greatest strength is your practical common sense. You need contact with beautiful things— man-made or natural—and your feet need to be on the ground. Although sweet-natured, you can be stubborn when you feel threatened or insecure. Others may be quicker to start a journey, but you are the one who will reliably reach your destination.

THE PLANETS

We refer to the Sun and Moon as planets. Don't worry; we do know about modern astronomy. Although the Sun is really a star and the Moon is a satellite, they are called planets for astrological purposes. The astrological planets are the Sun, the Moon, Mercury, Venus, Mars, Jupiter, Saturn, Chiron, Uranus, Neptune, and Pluto.

Your sun sign is the most obvious astrological placement, for the Sun returns to the same sign every year. But at the same time, the Moon is orbiting the Earth, changing signs every two and a third days. Mercury, Venus, and Mars each move through a sign in a few weeks to a few months.

Jupiter spends a whole year in a sign—and Pluto visits a sign for up to 30 years! The ever-changing positions of the planets alter the energetic terrain through which we travel. The planets are symbols; each has a particular range of meanings. For example, Venus is the goddess of love, but it really symbolizes beauty in a spectrum of experiences. Venus can represent romantic love, sensuality, the arts, or good food. It activates anything that we value, including personal possessions and even money. To our ancestors, the planets actually animated life on Earth. In this way of thinking, every beautiful flower contains the essence of Venus.

Each sign has a natural affinity to an individual planet, and as this planet moves through the sky, it sends messages of particular interest to people born under that sign. Your key or ruling planet is Venus, the Greek goddess of love, beauty, pleasure, and fine objects. Its movement shows where self-worth and relationship issues, the principles of attraction and desire, and money come into your life, as well as times when you're open to receiving gifts. Planets can be described by many different words, for the mythology of each is a rich tapestry. In this book we use a variety of words when talking about each planet in order to convey the most applicable meaning. The table below describes a few keywords for each planet, including the Sun and Moon.

PLANET	SYMBOL	KEYWORDS
Sun	☉	Consciousness, Will, Vitality
Moon	☽	Subconscious, Emotions, Habits
Mercury	☿	Communication, Thoughts, Transportation
Venus	♀	Desire, Love, Money, Values
Mars	♂	Action, Physical Energy, Drive
Jupiter	♃	Expansion, Growth, Optimism
Saturn	♄	Contraction, Maturity, Responsibility
Chiron	⚷	Healing, Pain, Subversion
Uranus	♅	Awakening, Unpredictable, Inventive
Neptune	♆	Imagination, Spirituality, Confusion
Pluto	♇	Passion, Intensity, Regeneration

HOUSES

Just as planets move through the signs of the zodiac, they also move through the houses in an individual chart. The 12 houses correspond to the 12 signs, but are individualized, based upon your sign. In this book we use Solar Houses, which place your sun sign in your 1st House. Therefore, when a planet enters a new sign it also enters a new house. If you know your exact time of birth, the rising sign determines the 1st House. You can learn your rising sign by entering your birth date at:

http://www.tarot.com/astrology/astroprofile

HOUSE	SIGN	KEYWORDS
1st House	Aries	Self, Appearance, Personality
2nd House	Taurus	Possessions, Values, Self-Worth
3rd House	Gemini	Communication, Siblings, Short Trips
4th House	Cancer	Home, Family, Roots
5th House	Leo	Love, Romance, Children, Play
6th House	Virgo	Work, Health, Daily Routines
7th House	Libra	Marriage, Relationships, Business Partners
8th House	Scorpio	Intimacy, Transformation, Shared Resources
9th House	Sagittarius	Travel, Higher Education, Philosophy
10th House	Capricorn	Career, Community, Ambition
11th House	Aquarius	Groups and Friends, Associations, Social Ideals
12th House	Pisces	Imagination, Spirituality, Secret Activities

ASPECTS

As the planets move through the sky in their various cycles, they form ever-changing angles with one another. Certain angles create significant geometric shapes. So, when two planets are 90 degrees apart, they conform to a square; 60 degrees of separation conforms to a sextile, or six-pointed star. Planets create **aspects** when they're at these special angles. Aspects explain how the individual symbolism of pairs of planets combine into an energetic pattern.

ASPECT	DEGREES	KEYWORDS
Conjunction	0	Compression, Blending, Focus
Opposition	180	Tension, Awareness, Balance
Trine	120	Harmony, Free-Flowing, Ease
Square	90	Resistance, Stress, Dynamic Conflict
Quintile	72	Creativity, Metaphysical, Magic
Sextile	60	Support, Intelligent, Activating
Quincunx	150	Irritation, Annoyance, Adjustment

2009 GENERAL FORECAST:
THE INDIVIDUAL AND THE COLLECTIVE

Astrology works for individuals, groups, and even humanity as a whole. You will have your own story in 2009, but it will unfold among seven billion other tales of human experience in the year ahead. We are each unique, yet our lives touch one another; our destinies are woven together by weather and war, by economy, science, politics, religion, and all the other threads of life on this planet. We make personal choices every day, yet there are great events beyond the control of any one individual. When the power goes out in a neighborhood, it affects everyone, yet individual astrology patterns will describe the personal response of each person. Our existence is both an individual and collective experience.

We are living at a time when the tools of self-awareness fill bookshelves, Web sites, and broadcasts, and we benefit greatly from them. Yet despite all this wisdom, conflicts among groups cause enormous suffering every day. Understanding personal issues is a powerful means for increasing happiness, but knowledge of our collective issues is equally important for our safety, sanity, and well-being. This astrological look at the major trends and planetary patterns for 2009 provides a framework for understanding the potentials and challenges we face together, so that we can advance with tolerance and respect as a community and fulfill our potentials as individuals.

The astrological events used for this forecast are the transits of major planets Jupiter and Saturn, the retrograde cycles of Mercury, and the eclipses of the Sun and the Moon.

A NOTE ABOUT THE DATES IN THIS BOOK

All events are based upon the Eastern Time Zone of the United States. Because of local time differences, an event occurring just minutes after midnight in the East will actually happen the prior day in the rest of the country. Although the key dates are the exact dates of any particular alignment, some of you are so ready for certain things to happen that you can react to a transit a day or two before it is exact. And sometimes you could be so entrenched in habits or unwilling to change that you may not notice the effects right away. Allow extra time around each key date to feel the impact of any event.

JUPITER IN AQUARIUS
COLLECTIVE CONSCIOUSNESS
January 5, 2009–January 17, 2010

Expansive Jupiter enters inventive and idealistic Aquarius, opening our minds to unexpected possibilities and futuristic visions for reorganizing society. Philosophical, religious, and political boundaries are crossed as new combinations of beliefs evolve, replacing outmoded ideologies. The importance of teamwork and cooperation increases as generous Jupiter in group-oriented Aquarius challenges existing hierarchies and dysfunctional authorities. Growing awareness of the interconnectedness of all living creatures favors a holistic view of reality in which environmental issues and unequal distribution of resources can be addressed more effectively.

Jupiter and Aquarius are both associated with mental activity, making this a rich time for breakthroughs in brain research. Practices for developing the mind become popular as baby boomers strive to stay sharp and recent discoveries spur innovative approaches to education. Technology should advance rapidly, especially if it involves networks—an area associated with Aquarius. Yet there is a shadow side to all this intellectual firepower, for both Jupiter and Aquarius have the potential to "know it all." The desire to have all the answers is a driving force for human exploration—even as it can engender hubris and an assumption of infallibility that both negate discussion or compromise. Fortunately, such tendencies are tempered this year by Jupiter's conjunctions with Neptune and Chiron.

Neptune is the planet of compassion and spirituality, representing the boundless field of feeling that lies beyond the limits of the mind. Chiron is the Wounded Healer, a reminder of the value of vulnerability in salving the pain of mortality. Jupiter conjuncts Neptune on May 27, July 10, and December 21 and joins Chiron on May 23, July 22, and December 21. The super-conjunction of Jupiter, Neptune, and Chiron creates a rare mix of awareness on all levels that can go a long way toward opening individual and collective consciousness. We may begin to see ourselves in a new light with greater understanding of our potential and purpose.

SATURN IN VIRGO
LEAVE NO STONE UNTURNED
September 2, 2007–October 29, 2009

Saturn, the planet of boundaries and limitations, takes twenty-nine years to orbit the Sun and pass through all twelve signs of the zodiac. It demands serious responsibility, shows the work needed to overcome obstacles, and teaches us how to build new structures in our lives. Saturn thrives on patience and commitment, rewarding well-planned and persistent effort but punishing sloppiness with delay, disappointment, and failure. Saturn's passage through detail-oriented Virgo is a time to perfect skills, cut waste, and develop healthier habits. Saturn and Virgo are both pragmatic, which makes them an excellent pair for improving the quality of material life. Bodies can be more susceptible to illnesses caused by impure food or water, making this an ideal time to improve your diet. Environmental issues grow in importance as we approach a critical point in the relationship between humanity and planet Earth. Fortunately, Saturn in exacting Virgo is excellent for cleaning up unhealthy toxins produced by old technologies and in leading the way to create new ecologically friendly systems for the future.

Saturn in Virgo highlights flaws and makes it easier to be critical of yourself and others. Yet its true purpose is to solve problems, not simply complain about them. Small steps in a positive direction can slowly build to a tidal wave of improvement wherever you place your attention this year.

SATURN IN LIBRA
TESTING RELATIONSHIPS
October 29, 2009–October 5, 2012

Saturn's shift into peace-loving Libra marks a new chapter in all kinds of relationships. Cooperation and civility allow diplomacy to flourish as reason replaces force. The need to weigh both sides of any argument can slow down personal and public dialogue, yet it's worth the price to build bridges over seemingly impassable chasms. Saturn is "exalted" in Libra according to astrological tradition, suggesting a highly positive link between the planet's principle of integrity and Libra's sense of fair play. The negative side of Saturn, though, is its potential for rigidity, which can manifest now as a stubborn unwillingness to listen. Resistance to opposing points of view is simply a test of their worth; only with careful consideration can they be properly evaluated. Responsible individuals and leaders recognize the importance of treating others as equals as a foundation for any healthy relationship.

MERCURY RETROGRADES
January 11–February 1 in Aquarius / May 2–May 30 in Gemini / September 7–September 29 in Libra

All true planets appear to move retrograde from time to time as a result of being viewed from the moving platform of Earth. The most significant retrograde periods are those of Mercury, the communication planet. Occurring three times a year for roughly three weeks at a time, these are periods when difficulties with details, travel, information flow, and technical matters are likely.

Although Mercury's retrograde phase has received a fair amount of bad press, it isn't necessarily a negative cycle. Because personal and commercial interactions are emphasized, you can actually accomplish more than usual, especially if you stay focused on what needs to be done rather than initiating new projects. But you may feel as if you're treading water—or worse yet, carried backward in an undertow of unfinished business. Worry less about making progress than about the quality of your work. Extra attention should be paid to all your communication exchanges. Avoiding omissions and misunderstandings is the ideal way to preemptively deal with unnecessary complications. Retrograde Mercury is best used to tie up loose ends as you review, redo, reconsider, and, in general, revisit the past.

This year, the three retrogrades are in intellectual air signs (Aquarius, Gemini, and Libra), which can be very useful for analysis and remedial studies that help you reevaluate what you already know so you can take your learning to the next level.

ECLIPSES
Solar: January 26 and July 21
Lunar: February 9, July 7, August 5, and December 31

Solar and Lunar Eclipses are special New and Full
Moons that indicate meaningful changes for individuals
and groups. They are powerful markers of events
whose influences can appear up to three months in
advance and last up to six months afterward.

January 26, Solar Eclipse in Aquarius: Society of the Future

Eclipses are usually about endings, but this one has plenty of propulsion to drive forward new ideas and organizations. Opportunistic Jupiter is conjunct the eclipse to seed minds with vision far into the future. Loving Venus is joined with Uranus, Aquarius's ingenious ruling planet, revealing fresh forms for relationships and uncommon aesthetics. Stern Saturn's opposition to this unconventional pair could stifle expression, but a constructive trine from industrious Mars in Capricorn helps overcome any resistance.

February 9, Lunar Eclipse in Leo: Cosmic Community

A Lunar Eclipse in dramatic Leo cuts egos down to size, turning brilliant stars into black holes and overinflated winners into losers. The appearance of loss, however, may be obscured by nebulous Neptune's conjunction with the Sun and opposition to the Moon, allowing illusion and deception to cover up failures. The upside of this event is an awakening to the connectedness of all living things. Spiritual Neptune in collectivist Aquarius reveals identity beyond personal ego, opening individuals and groups to communities of soul and service. Let pride dissolve in waters of compassion while moving from fields of competition to webs of cooperation. Philosophical Jupiter's close conjunction with the integrative Lunar North Node promises wisdom, while energetic Mars can turn ideas into action.

July 7, *Lunar Eclipse in Capricorn: Realigning Responsibilities*

This Lunar Eclipse in Capricorn chips away at emotional defenses, revealing gentler ways to manage daily life. The overly ambitious and excessively disciplined may be diverted from their well-defined paths to address personal issues. The usual insecurities associated with an eclipse in traditional Capricorn are lessened by a supportive trine from Saturn. This provides a safety rail of relative stability through this wobbly time. Examine the rules you've created for yourself and consider dropping those that no longer serve your needs. Reducing extraneous obligations can help you focus on the tasks and goals most vital for you right now.

July 21, *Solar Eclipse in Cancer: Cutting the Cord*

This Solar Eclipse in the last degree of nostalgic Cancer can produce a flood of memories, pulling your attention back to the past. Yet this is no time to linger over photo albums, souvenirs, and thoughts of love found and lost. Say good-bye to self-protective habits that inhibit growth and block fulfillment. Independent Uranus forms a supportive trine to the eclipse, suddenly making it easier to cut loose what's no longer needed. Nurturing the future, rather than the past, is the gift of this significant event. The eclipse is visible in central China and India, making these countries prime candidates for dramatic change.

August 5, Lunar Eclipse in Aquarius: The Kid in You
It's rare that Lunar Eclipses arrive two months in a row, making this summer a period of major transformation. This event in intellectual Aquarius challenges us to come down from ivory towers and act on our innovative ideas. The Sun in bold Leo opposite the Moon indicates the need for courage and a willingness to take risks. Fortunately, assertive Mars in versatile Gemini shows a variety of paths that can lead to success. Quick fixes and last-minute adjustments are easier with a friendly attitude more interested in enjoying the game than in the final score. When heads are made heavy by theory or competition, it's time for the child's heart to appear to bring playfulness to the party.

December 31, Lunar Eclipse in Cancer:
Tough Choices

This Lunar Eclipse in the Moon's own sign of nurturing Cancer can stir deep waters within families and close friendships. Potent Pluto opposes the Moon while strict Saturn squares it, creating tightness and pressure that can be frightening. It's tempting to duck confrontation or avoid any serious change; yet refusing to act only reduces your power. You may have hard choices to make on the cusp of the New Year, but they demand focus and clear intention—powerful allies for redefining life. Sweet Venus in dutiful Capricorn is between Pluto and the Sun, opposite the Moon, tempting you to do anything to maintain appearances. Still, the prizes of fulfillment go to those brave enough to face outer reality and inner desire without flinching.

Remember that all of these astrological events are part of the general cosmic weather for the year, but will affect us each differently based upon our individual astrological signs.

TAURUS
AUGUST–DECEMBER
2008 OVERVIEW

LET GO OF THE PAST

This month begins with a powerful roar as the New Moon on **August 1** eclipses the relentless Leo Sun in your 4th House of Home and Family. Personal issues move to the forefront, distracting you from your work. The real message here, however, is to acknowledge the importance of your roots, although family ties may produce their share of stressful situations. A fresh perspective can wash away past negativity, preparing you for the changes ahead, especially within the context of relationships. Emotions intensify early in the month as innocent Venus dances into the shadows of Pluto on **August 5.** The focus of your desires narrows as Venus enters discerning Virgo on **August 6,** but your need to communicate exactly what you want grows until mental Mercury trines Pluto on **August 9,** then slips into Virgo on **August 10.**

Fluctuating moods can complicate your life as sensual Venus and intellectual Mercury run into Saturn's austerity, forcing you to consider solitude as a viable alternative to the overwhelming confusion of love. But your isolation is temporary, for the Aquarius Full Moon Eclipse on **August 16** draws your energy from the subjective personal realms into the more objective issues of community and career. Venus harmonizes with opulent Jupiter, so the rewards will be yours if you have done your homework and learned your lessons well. Still, you may have to fight for what's important as combative Mars crosses swords with powerful Pluto on **August 17.** A second New Moon on **August 30** is in efficient Virgo, telling you to take responsibility for the life you have created for yourself. Oddly enough, it can be lots of fun if you're willing to work for it.

FRIDAY 1

SATURDAY 2

SUNDAY 3

MONDAY 4

TUESDAY 5 ★ Intensity creates results through the 6th

WEDNESDAY 6 ★

THURSDAY 7

FRIDAY 8

SATURDAY 9

SUNDAY 10

MONDAY 11

TUESDAY 12

WEDNESDAY 13 ★ SUPER NOVA DAYS Love turns lemons into lemonade
through the 17th

THURSDAY 14 ★

FRIDAY 15 ★

SATURDAY 16 ★

SUNDAY 17 ★

MONDAY 18

TUESDAY 19

WEDNESDAY 20

THURSDAY 21 ★ Make positive changes through the 24th. Satisfaction is worth
the wait

FRIDAY 22 ★

SATURDAY 23 ★

SUNDAY 24 ★

MONDAY 25

TUESDAY 26

WEDNESDAY 27

THURSDAY 28

FRIDAY 29 ★ Rediscover harmony by establishing balance through the 30th

SATURDAY 30 ★

SUNDAY 31

NARROW YOUR FOCUS

September begins as a rather serious month, yet your desire to accomplish your goals is balanced by the encouragement you receive and the very real progress you make. The powerful planetary regulators, optimistic Jupiter and realistic Saturn, form a harmonious trine on **September 8.** Their stabilizing influence is palpable and greatly impacts the remainder of the year, replaying a familiar theme from their previous trine in late January. You may get a taste of Saturn's severity on **September 3,** followed by Jupiter's benevolence on **September 4,** filling you with pride about the work you do and the promises you keep. But there are countercurrents that arise as Mercury, Venus, and Mars travel together as a pack through fair-minded Libra. Between **September 7 and September 9,** they each square Jupiter, tempting you with unrealistic expectations and upsetting the otherwise healthy balance between ambition and achievement.

A series of irritating quincunxes from these same planets in your 6th House of Daily Routines to unorthodox Uranus from **September 16–19** can provoke rebellion if others attempt to rein in your uncharacteristically disobedient behavior. The wild Full Moon in escapist Pisces on **September 15** is conjunct Uranus and can drive you even closer to doing something you may later regret, relish, or both. The Autumnal Equinox on **September 22** marks the Sun's entrance into "team player" Libra and your 6th House of Work, showing your willingness to labor quietly behind the scenes now. Lovely Venus turns secretive as it enters the hidden worlds of passionate Scorpio on **September 23.** Restless Mercury begins its three-week retrograde on **September 24,** reemphasizing this inward shift. The creative Libra New Moon in your 6th House on **September 29** can help focus your mind on the tasks ahead.

MONDAY 1

TUESDAY 2

WEDNESDAY 3 ★ Balance your cautious attitude with an open mind through the 4th

THURSDAY 4 ★

FRIDAY 5

SATURDAY 6

SUNDAY 7

MONDAY 8

TUESDAY 9 ★ Save your strength for long-term goals through the 11th

WEDNESDAY 10 ★

THURSDAY 11 ★

FRIDAY 12

SATURDAY 13

SUNDAY 14

MONDAY 15 ★ **SUPER NOVA DAYS** Fuel your dreams with reality through the 19th

TUESDAY 16 ★

WEDNESDAY 17 ★

THURSDAY 18 ★

FRIDAY 19 ★

SATURDAY 20

SUNDAY 21

MONDAY 22 ★ A journey into your fears is fruitful through the 24th

TUESDAY 23 ★

WEDNESDAY 24 ★

THURSDAY 25

FRIDAY 26

SATURDAY 27

SUNDAY 28

MONDAY 29

TUESDAY 30

TAKE YOUR TIME

The devil is in the details with picky Mercury moving through your 6th House of Work all month and retrograde until **October 15.** You may be asked to go back over a job that you already considered finished; making progress can be difficult until Mercury turns direct in the middle of the month. You could even feel trapped by your daily routine with its emphasis on getting every task done right, especially since you'd rather be doing more exciting things. You should notice a change of pace when Mars moves into passionate Scorpio on **October 4** and someone enters your life on a whirlwind of emotional intensity. Your key planet, Venus, harmoniously contacts both ambitious Saturn and confident Jupiter between **October 5 and October 7.** Don't coast through this period, but take advantage of the stabilizing results you can obtain just by being extra helpful. Venus awakens your creativity and activates your fantasy life when it harmonizes with unconventional Uranus on **October 10** and squares dreamy Neptune on **October 11.**

The enthusiastic Aries Full Moon on **October 14** falls in your 12th House of Secrets and is supported by a sextile from Neptune. Focus on developing compassion and seeking ways to express yourself more spiritually, in particular through service to others. Your world becomes brighter when Venus flies into adventurous Sagittarius on **October 18,** showing you new ways to enjoy yourself. The Sun's entry into Scorpio on **October 22** reminds you to stay aware of other people's feelings, even while you are having fun. The powerful Scorpio New Moon on **October 28** falls in your 7th House of Partnerships, intensifying your emotions and perhaps even changing the dynamics of your current relationships.

WEDNESDAY 1

THURSDAY 2

FRIDAY 3

SATURDAY 4

SUNDAY 5 ★ Big ideas require hard work through the 7th

MONDAY 6 ★

TUESDAY 7 ★

WEDNESDAY 8

THURSDAY 9

FRIDAY 10 ★ You're off the beaten path. Stay open to surprises through the 11th

SATURDAY 11 ★

SUNDAY 12

MONDAY 13

TUESDAY 14 ★ Aim high! The pleasure is in the journey ahead through the 18th

WEDNESDAY 15 ★

THURSDAY 16 ★

FRIDAY 17 ★

SATURDAY 18 ★

SUNDAY 19

MONDAY 20

TUESDAY 21

WEDNESDAY 22

THURSDAY 23

FRIDAY 24

SATURDAY 25

SUNDAY 26

MONDAY 27

TUESDAY 28 ★ **SUPER NOVA DAYS** Make intimacy count through the 31st

WEDNESDAY 29 ★

THURSDAY 30 ★

FRIDAY 31 ★

CATERPILLAR INTO A BUTTERFLY

November gets off to a rather rocky start as Venus in adventurous Sagittarius forms simultaneous squares to both karmic Saturn and rebellious Uranus. In an irrepressible expression of your true desires, resistance gives way as you blast into the future. Saturn and Uranus are in exact opposition on **November 4,** establishing a theme for change through next summer. Responsible Saturn in your 5th House of Play makes you more serious in love and more authoritative in your relationships with kids. But its opposition to eccentric Uranus also creates tension around the enforcement of rules, tempting you to help others break free of any expectations that hold them back. On **November 12,** beautiful Venus slips into the shadows, joining mysterious Pluto in urging you to express your deepest desires. Venus enters earthy Capricorn later the same day, giving you a more practical orientation to love and money throughout the remainder of the month.

The indulgent Taurus Full Moon on **November 13** brings confusion, as its square to Neptune incites fantasy, overwhelming you with unrealistic dreams. Meanwhile, the regulators, expansive Jupiter and contractive Saturn, move into their third and final harmonizing trine this year on **November 21,** giving a clear sense of reality for you to successfully reach your goals. The Sun and Mercury enter philosophical Sagittarius on **November 21 and November 23,** respectively, motivating you to widen your vision and to move beyond simplistic objectives. Pluto enters strategic Capricorn on **November 26,** followed by the Sagittarius New Moon on **November 27,** giving you a new sense of confidence and indicating a long-term metamorphosis of your entire life.

SATURDAY 1

SUNDAY 2

MONDAY 3 ★ **SUPER NOVA DAYS** Be careful of impulsive actions through the 5th

TUESDAY 4 ★

WEDNESDAY 5 ★

THURSDAY 6

FRIDAY 7

SATURDAY 8

SUNDAY 9

MONDAY 10 ★ Be true to yourself through the 13th

TUESDAY 11 ★

WEDNESDAY 12 ★

THURSDAY 13 ★

FRIDAY 14

SATURDAY 15

SUNDAY 16 ★ Think realistically and success will materialize through the 18th

MONDAY 17 ★

TUESDAY 18 ★

WEDNESDAY 19

THURSDAY 20

FRIDAY 21

SATURDAY 22

SUNDAY 23

MONDAY 24

TUESDAY 25

WEDNESDAY 26

THURSDAY 27 ★ Return to common sense and take life seriously through the 29th

FRIDAY 28 ★

SATURDAY 29 ★

SUNDAY 30

POWER AND PLEASURE

December begins well and ends on an even higher note, yet you may run into conflict toward the middle of the month with lingering intensity throughout the holidays. Beautiful Venus hooks up with abundant Jupiter in Capricorn on **December 1** for what may be considered the sweetest possible aspect. This indicator of pleasurable sensuality is highlighted by the Moon—also in the serious sign of Capricorn—placing a slight damper on your otherwise highly indulgent activities. The results can be quite rewarding if you focus your intentions toward reaching long-term goals instead of only on receiving immediate gratification.

Venus enters smart Aquarius on **December 7**, remaining there for the rest of the year, encouraging you to break free from social conventions and explore more individualized expressions of your heart. Meanwhile, a countercurrent develops as thoughtful Mercury tells you to play life by the rules, entering methodical Capricorn on **December 12,** followed by the Sun on **December 21,** and Mars on **December 27.** The Gemini Full Moon in your 2nd House of Money, also on **December 12,** stresses the unresolved tensions from last month's Saturn-Uranus opposition. This can be unsettling, stretching your finances to the max or shaking your self-confidence with an emotional interaction that doesn't go your way. With the Sun conjunct assertive Mars, it's crucial to avoid letting a small disagreement escalate into declared war. The cautious Capricorn New Moon on **December 27** is counterbalanced by Venus's conjunction with nebulous Neptune. This awakens your spiritual needs—in stark contrast with required holiday activities, which may be less than inspirational. A transformational Mars-Pluto conjunction on **December 28** can stir passions as you take dramatic steps to set your course for the year ahead.

MONDAY 1 ★ Indulge yourself when old investments or efforts pay off

TUESDAY 2

WEDNESDAY 3

THURSDAY 4

FRIDAY 5

SATURDAY 6

SUNDAY 7 ★ Stay open to unusual experiences—today is a good day to experiment

MONDAY 8

TUESDAY 9

WEDNESDAY 10 ★ SUPER NOVA DAYS Make small changes to avoid a blow-up

THURSDAY 11 ★

FRIDAY 12 ★

SATURDAY 13 ★

SUNDAY 14 ★

MONDAY 15 ★

TUESDAY 16

WEDNESDAY 17

THURSDAY 18

FRIDAY 19

SATURDAY 20

SUNDAY 21 ★ Ride your ambition through the 23rd, but stay mindful of others

MONDAY 22 ★

TUESDAY 23 ★

WEDNESDAY 24

THURSDAY 25

FRIDAY 26

SATURDAY 27 ★ Look at your assumptions with a beginner's mind

SUNDAY 28 ★

MONDAY 29

TUESDAY 30

WEDNESDAY 31

2009 HOROSCOPE

TAURUS

APRIL 20–MAY 20

OVERVIEW OF THE YEAR

The stark contrast between your dreams of a more fulfilling future and the demands of daily life can pull you back and forth between hope and surrender this year. Optimistic Jupiter in your 10th House of Career expands your professional horizons with promises of greater responsibility and recognition. **An open-minded attitude is essential to reach these heights, because you're forced out of your comfort zone to encounter new and unconventional ways of doing business.** Jupiter's conjunctions with spiritual Neptune on May 27, July 10, and December 21 reveal creative ways to express your highest ideals through your job. Still, the balloon of hope can float so high that it seems always beyond your grasp. Think of this vision as a model meant to motivate you, rather than a fixed target you must reach to succeed. **You may have to step back from the concrete Taurus sense of reality** that expects tangible results to recognize that simply aspiring to greatness is a significant achievement.

A Solar Eclipse in socially conscious Aquarius activating your 10th House on January 26 is enriched by a conjunction with Jupiter while Venus, your ruling planet, is joined with inventive Uranus. **You may experience a sudden awakening to a totally new professional path.** Yet a Lunar Eclipse in Leo on February 9 opposing nebulous Neptune could trick you into believing in a fantasy that might never come true. Imagine, dream, and hope—but gather and absorb information, analyzing it before committing yourself to radical change. Venus turns retrograde in your secretive 12th House on March 6, giving you a chance to review key relationship issues before the love planet turns direct on April 17. Another Lunar Eclipse in your 10th House on August 5 is supported by a harmonious trine from busy Mars in Gemini, enabling you to take steps in a new direction without abandoning the safety and security of what you've already built.

Saturn, the planet of contraction and limits, is in your 6th House of Employment until October 29, anchoring your aspirations with discipline—or burying them under the weight of petty details and mundane tasks. **It's essential that you**

operate with greater efficiency on the job and in routine matters to gain enough time to advance your larger interests. If you match your high hopes with training and dedication, you might even catch that elusive balloon. Hardworking Saturn, though, began a series of tense oppositions with Uranus, the planet of surprise and independence, last November that will repeat on February 5, September 15, and through the summer of 2010. The stress between Saturn sticking to business in practical Virgo and rebellious Uranus in Pisces's yearning for freedom may provoke a desire to give up your ambitions and run away from it all. These aspects are reminders that **you will need breaks from the pressure to perform at a peak level**. Forcing yourself to plod along without taking time off can lead to a breakdown—quitting a job, abandoning your goals, or creating a conflict over control that ends your project.

THOU SHALT PLAY

You can expect a mature approach to love with serious Saturn in your 5th House of Romance through late October. You will benefit by making a concerted effort to enhance your image, but that doesn't come from hard work alone. Having fun gives you an attractive glow. Joy is part of your job now and needs to be on your schedule. Commit to activities that help you feel young and expressive. These traits are necessities, not luxuries, of love. The downside of Saturn in this part of your chart brings feelings of isolation or emotional fatigue that tempt you to give up on love. Happily, spontaneous Uranus's oppositions to Saturn on February 5 and September 15 should end your funk. Venus's retrograde period of March 6–April 17 is a critical time to reexamine core patterns in matters of love, partnership, and self-worth. Her passage through the haze of your 12th House of Secrets can stir up hidden feelings. Discovering these needs can challenge you to approach intimacy in new and different ways.

OPPORTUNITY KNOCKS

Generous Jupiter in your 10th House of Status can earn you a higher profile professionally this year. Flexible thinking and being a good team player are keys to taking advantage of this planetary opportunity. No matter how right you believe you are, remaining open to alternative points of view is vital for harmony with colleagues, clients, and even the general public. Success now comes from exploring uncharted waters and permitting inventiveness and intuition to guide you as much as common sense. Jupiter's conjunctions with dreamy Neptune on May 27, July 10, and December 21 might transport you to Fantasyland, so be careful about the commitments you make at these times. You will be uplifted by your idealism, yet can be so carried away by it that you lose sight of the basic principles that have brought you this far.

NO-SPECULATION ZONE

Over the long term, your finances look reasonably solid. Still, with Jupiter, the ruler of your 8th House of Shared Resources, conjuncting spacey Neptune three times this year, you should avoid speculative investments and unsecured loans. Financially astute Venus, your key planet, is retrograde March 6–April 17, hampering your usually sharp sense of value. Steer clear of significant financial commitments during this period of economic uncertainty. Additionally, Mercury, the ruler of your 2nd House of Resources, is retrograde May 6–June 30, demanding cautious money management to eliminate any questionable purchases and errors in paperwork.

GENTLE STRETCH

Venus is the planetary ruler of both Taurus and your 6th House of Health and Habits, making her retrograde period of March 6–April 17 one of your most physically vulnerable times of the year. Retreat from the world to rest, recuperate, and focus on your own needs rather than draining yourself with too much work and play. Energetic Mars is in Taurus from May 31 through July 11— a time when you have more energy to burn and increased stamina. A lack of exercise can leave you irritated, but overexertion can be counterproductive. Establish a regular pattern of movement that gently stretches your muscles and increases your endurance rather than trying to do too much, too fast.

REASONABLE EXPANSION

You're likely to see big movement on the home front this summer as two Sun-Moon conjunctions touch the domestic section of your chart. A Solar Eclipse on July 21 forms an expressive trine with innovative Uranus, bringing fresh ideas that make renovation, relocation, or family issues easier to handle than expected. The Leo New Moon on August 20 opposes optimistic Jupiter and fanciful Neptune, dramatizing emotions and stirring your dreams of a grander living place. Fortunately, agile Mars in Gemini's supportive trine to these giant planets guides you to intelligently maneuver through crises and enhance your environment without going overboard.

PLAY IT SAFE

Transformative Pluto's long-term transit of your 9th House of Travel opens you to life-changing journeys this year. A tense Jupiter-Pluto semisquare on March 27 and edgy Mars-Pluto opposition on August 26 could complicate trips, however, so be extra cautious if you are planning to be on the road. Back away from stressful situations that could escalate if you add fuel to the fire. Education, whether formal or not, works best this year when you favor practice over theory. Abstract ideas without direct application can be fascinating, but are not the optimal use of your mental and physical resources.

DEEP DIVING

Psychic activity and spiritual awareness churn into
high gear on March 8 when Mars, the ruler of your
12th House of Soul Consciousness, joins other-
worldly Neptune. The fiery Aries New Moon in this
house on March 26 is in a heated square with
intense Pluto, which could help you release deeply
held fears and desires. Bringing them to the surface is healthy as long as you don't allow them to
overpower you. Seek support or step back from
the emotional edge if you feel unsafe. Mars
sextiles the spiritually rich Jupiter-Neptune conjunction on May 26, opening your heart and soul
to inspiring ideas and exhilarating experiences.

RICK & JEFF'S TIP FOR THE YEAR
When You Win, We All Win

Elevated aspirations, self-discipline, and hard work are your major allies this year. Instead of battling to maintain your present position in life, you might as well aim as high as you can. It won't take much more effort to achieve greatness, so why not go for the biggest prizes you can imagine? A bit of idealism is the secret sauce that can turn your personal desires into reality. Recognizing the connection between your own ambitions and benefits to humanity as a whole turns your individual success into a collective gain. With this picture vividly in mind, you can attract the kind of friendly support that makes even the toughest tasks manageable and pleasant.

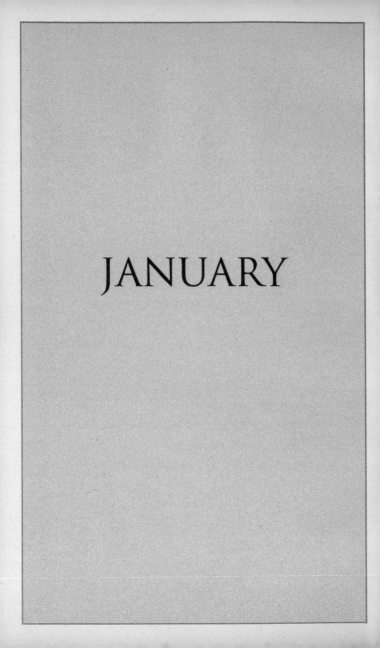

JANUARY

PROFESSIONAL REDIRECTION

Expansive Jupiter moves into your 10th House of Career on **January 5**, opening your mind to a broader vision of your professional future. An inspiring idea can nudge you to seek a higher purpose in your present job or expose you to a fresh concept that could lead you into a totally new field. The illuminating Full Moon in sensitive Cancer on **January 10** casts its light on your 3rd House of Information, where facts and feelings mix to intensify conversations and deepen your curiosity. Yet insecurities can trigger arguments where trust has been eroded by uncertainty. Backing off from your habitual emotional reactions can reveal the true source of your behavior and make different choices possible. Communicative Mercury turns retrograde on **January 11**, which can complicate matters at work through the end of the month. Crossed signals, lost data, and equipment failure may be more common, so double-check details to reduce confusion and lost time.

The Sun's entry into intelligent Aquarius and your 10th House on **January 19** can raise your public profile and enhance your leadership status. Adjusting to new responsibilities could be a challenge, especially if you insist on doing everything the old way. Learning new methods and systems isn't easy with Mercury retrograde, but taking the time to retrain yourself means you'll be more efficient later. The Aquarius New Moon Eclipse on **January 26** could turn your work life upside down. Insatiable Jupiter contacts the ongoing opposition between restrictive Saturn and independent Uranus on **January 27–30**, which is unlikely to put you in the mood to compromise. The desire to do your own thing could cause conflict with an authority figure. Just have an alternative route to take if you burn any bridges.

KEEP IN MIND THIS MONTH

Pressuring yourself to act quickly will only push you farther off track. Patience is a slower but surer way to regain control of your life.

KEY DATES

★ **JANUARY 3-4**
pleasure hunt
Your ruling planet, Venus, enters spiritual
Pisces on **January 3**, softening your heart and
touching your soul. Making magic with friends
can wash away your worries in a sea of temporary pleasure and delight. Lose yourself in the
company of caring pals who ask little of you
but are willing to offer so much. A savvy sextile
between Venus and potent Pluto on **January 4**
gives you the power of gentle persuasion to
motivate others in subtle ways. Connections
deepen with an easy flow of feelings that draws
you closer as you discover hidden treasures
and talents in yourself and those around you.

★ **JANUARY 9-11**
ingenious applications
On **January 9**, the creative power of the Sun
aligns favorably with inventive Uranus on its
way to a harmonious trine with responsible
Saturn on **January 11**. The solar link between
these opposing planets gathers up original

ideas and flashes of intuition, blending them into a workable form to start making them real. Mental Mercury's retrograde turn on the **11th**, though, slows down this process of capturing lightning in a bottle. You may have to experiment with a variety of approaches before finding the right formula.

★ **JANUARY 17–18**
   all over the map
   Brainy Mercury skids into a 45-degree semi-square with eccentric Uranus on **January 17**, stirring up your nervous system and prompting strange conversations. The intellectual intensity of this high-frequency hookup grows even stronger when gigantic Jupiter brings a wave of information by joining the messenger planet on **January 18**. This union in unconventional Aquarius is enough to overwhelm anyone, especially during Mercury's quirky retrograde period. *Brilliant but erratic* describes the mental landscape as awesome insights mix with totally unrealistic ideas. You're swamped with speculations about future possibilities—just remember that your perception of down-

to-earth events could be sketchy now. Stay loose to keep from getting uptight about others' craziness or even your own unusual thoughts.

SUPER NOVA DAYS

★ **JANUARY 22–24**
relationship management
Vivacious Venus joins electric Uranus on **January 22**, bringing surprises to your style, taste, and relationships. You're restless enough to fire up conflict with an authority figure, so be ready to take bold action if you push issues to the limit. Serious negotiations with a partner or close friend are likely on **January 24**, when Venus opposes strict Saturn. Any tendencies to feel undervalued or hopeless are balanced by assertive Mars receiving supportive aspects from both Venus and Saturn. You'll handle complicated personal business with courage and maturity, reducing conflict and restoring your trust and confidence both in yourself and in those closest to you.

FEBRUARY

A GROWING SENSE OF COMMUNITY

Expect your long-term plans to crystallize when intellectual Mercury turns direct in your 9th House of Big Ideas on **February 1**. This provides a healthy balance between current needs and future possibilities that makes it safe to explore uncharted waters. Structuring Saturn's opposition to eccentric Uranus on **February 5** is the cornerstone of this unconventional month. This is the second in a series that began late last year and doesn't finish until **July 2010**. Still, patterns set now can determine whether you put yourself in a defensive position by digging in your heels and resisting change or find the will to take bold steps to create more freedom in your life. Connecting with friends or groups that motivate you to explore new experiences is an excellent way to move in a positive direction. Active Mars enters Uranus's home sign, Aquarius, on **February 4**, underscoring the importance of stepping out of your comfort zone. His passage through your 10th House of Career signals a need to try different methods if you want to advance professionally.

The Full Moon in lively Leo on **February 9** is a Lunar Eclipse in your 4th House of Home and Family. Emotional excess can trigger drama out of proportion with reality. Imaginative Neptune's opposition to the Full Moon makes it difficult to separate fact from fiction, but it also represents the presence of compassion that can heal all wounds. The spiritual Pisces New Moon on **February 24** warms you with the company of caring friends and inspires you with group activities that build a sense of community. Cultivating common cause with like-minded individuals multiplies your power, enabling you to affect your environment in ways you cannot achieve on your own.

KEEP IN MIND THIS MONTH

Pushing the limits of your potential can feel awkward at first. That doesn't mean it's the wrong thing to do.

KEY DATES

★ **FEBRUARY 2**
safety dance
Your ruling planet, Venus, enters fiery Aries, which tends to bring out your impulsive side—but it's in your 12th House of Escapism, where your decision making may not be at its best. Careless pursuit of pleasure can cost you more than you expect, yet your need for spontaneous fun is very real. Find ways to express this playful side of your personality without risk to yourself, your bank account, or an important relationship.

★ **FEBRUARY 4–5**
negotiating your worth
Mars's entry into Aquarius on **February 4** sparks an electric power intensified by the Saturn-Uranus opposition on **February 5**—yet both may be cloaked by the dark clouds of personal issues. Venus creates a tense semisquare with the Sun the same day that both planets form challenging aspects to potent Pluto, which can undermine trust and self-worth. Getting

what you want from others can be difficult—or
the price may be more than you are willing to
pay. Either way, it's healthier to discuss your
differences than to suffer in silence.

★ **FEBRUARY 11–12**
performance pressure
Aggressive Mars clashes with Saturn on
February 11 and Uranus the next day, which
can put you under great stress. Prioritize your
responsibilities, since meeting all of them right
now may not be possible. A fuzzy Sun-Neptune
conjunction on **February 12** can represent mis-
direction, where an authority figure leads you
astray or you take on a new role without proper
preparation. Avoid putting additional tasks on
your schedule until you are certain that your
current ones are under control.

SUPER NOVA DAYS

★ **FEBRUARY 16–18**
personality plus
A juicy Venus-Jupiter sextile on **February 16**
launches a festival of fast-and-furious fun and
productivity. This generous and ego-enhancing

aspect is followed by an enterprising conjunction between initiating Mars and visionary Jupiter on **February 17** that brings inventiveness and energy to the workplace. Attractive Venus forms a sweet sextile with Mars on **February 18**, highlighting your social skills and creative abilities. This happy hookup between the lover planets makes it easy to mix work and play; you may seem to be flirting even when you're not. Charm is indeed a powerful force in your personal and professional life, but use it carefully to avoid confusion. The Sun's entry into idealistic Pisces the same day adds another layer of fantasy that potentially blurs boundaries.

★ **FEBRUARY 24–25**
fireside chats
A brilliant conjunction between Mercury and Jupiter on **February 24** sparks bright ideas and scintillating conversations. Chatty Mercury's favorable sextile with loving Venus on **February 25** helps you turn routine tasks into pleasurable ones and difficult discussions into a caring and constructive exchanges of ideas.

MARCH

RELATIONSHIPS REDUX

You revisit old relationship, financial, and self-worth issues this month, for your ruling planet, Venus, turns retrograde on **March 6** and will continue her reversal until **April 17**. The cycle begins in the forward-leaning sign of Aries, indicating that looking back to the past will probably bring you a fresh perspective on where to go next to find love, pleasure, and approval. Don't defend old positions that no longer suit your current needs. Changing your mind is a sign of intelligence rather than weakness. The discerning Virgo Full Moon on **March 10** falls in your 5th House of Love and Play, which usually opens the door to pleasure. This time, though, stern Saturn conjuncts the Moon while unpredictable Uranus conjuncts the Sun, bringing the long-term opposition of these outer planets into the foreground. Restraint and rebellion battle for control as you find yourself holding back your feelings and then allowing them to explode. Emotional extremes are possible, especially with friends and lovers, so let the dust settle instead of making hasty decisions or shocking ultimatums.

The Sun's entry into enterprising Aries on **March 20** marks the Vernal Equinox, a seasonal shift that illuminates your spiritual 12th House. Retreating from the world—for a month or a minute—offers you a healthy balance, reducing the stress of daily life. The freshness of the Aries New Moon on **March 26** is tainted by a tense square from Pluto. The challenging presence of this transformational planet can evoke power struggles that are more about learning to let go than gaining control. Pluto's riches come from eliminating what's no longer needed so you can clear a space for New Moon seeds to take root and grow.

KEEP IN MIND THIS MONTH

The most important work you do this month is inner and private. Give yourself enough time alone to do it well.

KEY DATES

SUPER NOVA DAYS

★ **MARCH 6-8**
unchecked idealism
Protect yourself during these tender times as
Venus's retrograde turn on **March 6** is followed
by a vulnerable Mars-Neptune conjunction on
March 8 in your 10th House of Career and
Public Life. You can exhaust yourself trying to
complete impossible tasks. Ask for help if the
burden is too great, rather than pushing ahead
without the support you need. The Sun's opposition to rigid Saturn and Mercury's entry into
visionary Pisces increase your sense of obliga-
tion without the benefit of a practical point of
view. Still, it's fine to aim high as long as you
keep your feet on the ground.

★ **MARCH 14**
fork in the road
Relationships can take rocky turn when sweet
Venus forms a cranky semisquare with assertive
Mars just before the warrior planet enters
passive Pisces. An unsettled mood that shifts

between aggression and surrender is complicated by the Moon's passage through your 7th
House of Partnerships. Dealing intelligently with
strong feelings, though, can be the catalyst that
either strengthens a current connection or
shows you that it has reached its limit.

★ **MARCH 18–19**
finely tuned machine
Expect serious conversations with talkative
Mercury opposite disciplined Saturn on **March 18**.
Colleagues may be demanding and friends
less than friendly as you feel pressed to solve
problems on your own. Fortunately, a potent
Mars-Pluto sextile on **March 19** helps you
eliminate distractions and operate at a very
high level of efficiency to cut a big task down
to an easily manageable size.

★ **MARCH 22**
a glimpse of tomorrow
Wild ideas prove exciting, but not necessarily
practical. A mentally charged conjunction of
Mercury and Uranus cranks up originality while
tense aspects from the Sun to expansive

Jupiter and Venus to boundless Neptune replace reality with grand dreams. A slippery quincunx between hopeful Jupiter and doubting Saturn reflects the difficulty of making big plans stick. Theorizing and speculating, however, expand future possibilities, even if you're not ready to manifest them now.

★ **MARCH 27–28**
sweet persuasion
You see your beliefs challenged on **March 27** with an uncomfortable semisquare between Jupiter in idealistic Aquarius and Pluto in skeptical Capricorn. It's best not to get bogged down in philosophical, political, or religious debates, since emotions are stronger than reason. Mercury squares Pluto and semi-squares Jupiter to intensify your desire to prove your point. Pressure, though, only increases resistance; seek a more diplomatic way to influence others. Happily, gracious Venus forms conjunctions to the Sun on **March 27** and to Mercury on **March 28**. She shows you how to avoid conflict by applying charm, not force, to convey your message.

APRIL

PLEASURE PRINCIPLE

Intense feelings complicate the first weekend of the month as expressive Venus in Aries squares potent Pluto on **April 3**, one day before the tiny, distant planet turns retrograde. A fierce face-off between go-for-it Mars and no-go Saturn on **April 4** ratchets up tension. The slightest delay or alteration in plans can trigger fears out of proportion with the situation. You may in fact be sensing deeper issues about trust, safety, and intimacy that are better expressed dramatically than shoved back into the closet of denial. Mental Mercury's entry into dependable Taurus on **April 9** supports objective thinking and clear communication that adds authority to anything you say. The Libra Full Moon on the same day falls in your 6th House of Work and Service, highlighting imbalances that are undermining business relationships. However, optimistic Jupiter's happy trine to the Full Moon should bring you enough recognition, or hope for professional advancement, to keep you from feeling undervalued.

The Sun enters sensual Taurus on **April 19** to begin your season of birthday celebration. The sweet self-indulgence of your sign is worthy of a monthlong party for the senses. Yet solar pride and courage bring out your confident side, so put down the Ben & Jerry's to impress others with your boldness and creativity. The Taurus New Moon on **April 24** brings newfound awareness of your untapped inner resources. A dynamic trine from deep-diving Pluto to this Sun-Moon conjunction balances any Taurus tendency toward laziness with a desire to make the most of yourself. Travel, training, and education are ways to transform potential talents into practical tools for personal and professional growth.

KEEP IN MIND THIS MONTH

Follow your heart's desire and you can find diamonds of ability in yourself that simply need time and attention to fully develop.

KEY DATES

★ **APRIL 3-4**
at the crossroads
The rising emotions of romantic Venus stressed by demanding Pluto reveal deep layers of dissatisfaction on **April 3**. However, learning what doesn't work in your life can be a powerful first step toward meaningful change. Pluto's retrograde turn and the unrelenting Mars-Saturn opposition on **April 4** mark the end of one road and the beginning of another. Fortunately, an inventive sextile between fast-moving Mercury and philosophical Jupiter gives you the clarity to speak the truth without anger or guilt.

★ **APRIL 9-11**
realistic nostalgia
Thoughts turn serious as Mercury enters your sign and makes a challenging sesquisquare with Saturn on **April 9**. Expect difficulty with details and a need to explain yourself slowly to be understood. Your mood brightens with a generous Sun-Jupiter sextile on **April 10**,

pulling you out of the shadows and into the spotlight. Venus backpedals into sensitive Pisces on **April 11** to reawaken old romantic dreams and reconnect you with friends and groups who inspired you in the past.

★ APRIL 15–17
take a deep breath

A shocking Mars-Uranus conjunction in your 11th House of Friends and Associates on **April 15** stirs rebellion and spawns surprises. Trying to put a lid on the situation will only build up more steam, possibly leading to an explosion. Overcome your instinct to stifle change and allow as much movement as you can stand. Venus turns direct on **April 17** while strained by a semisquare from Mercury. Hypersensitivity can make innocent comments feel like major criticism, so it's wise to step back before responding.

SUPER NOVA DAYS

★ APRIL 21–24
burning love

Magnetic Venus meets passionate Mars in the last degree of psychic Pisces on **April 21**, and game playing becomes almost unavoidable. Flirting and teasing are too delicious to stop unless you invest this energy in a creative project instead. Mars rams into bold Aries on **April 22**, turning the heat up another notch before finally boiling over when Venus returns to the fire sign on **April 24**. You bubble with intensity during this sizzling time, swinging from extreme attraction to total rejection. Stay in the moment to keep things from getting out of hand. Consider this a free zone in which you have the right to explore without having to justify your behavior.

★ **APRIL 26**
damage control
Playtime is over as a deadly serious Mars-Pluto square sets the cost of carelessness too high. Put away distracting thoughts and focus on taking care of the essential business at hand. There is some vital cleaning up for you to do, and it can't wait until tomorrow.

MAY

LOOKING BACK ONE MORE TIME

Mercury—keeper of messages and master of details—turns retrograde on **May 7** in your 2nd House of Resources, which can lead to some backtracking on monetary matters. Avoid signing important papers or making significant financial investments until this Trickster turns direct on **May 30**. The passionate Scorpio Full Moon on **May 9** turns up the heat in your 7th House of Partnerships. A pushy square from strident Jupiter can overburden you at work or exaggerate philosophical differences with your other half. However, supportive aspects from solid Saturn and unorthodox Uranus add stability and original-ity, bringing a breath of fresh of air and broaden-ing the horizons of relationships.

On **May 13**, retrograde Mercury returns to Taurus, where it will stay until **June 13**. Its second visit to your sign gives you a chance to review recent decisions from a new perspective. Yet your fixed Taurus nature could lead you to simply dig in your heels and resist the new and strange. Notice whether you're reacting out of habit or standing up for a principle that's worth defending. Saturn turns direct on **May 16**, which usually indicates a good time to put plans into action. It's probably best to wait until skillful Mercury also goes direct next month, though, before making any serious commitment. The restless Gemini New Moon on **May 24** is a lively lunation that opens your mind to alternative sources of income and underdeveloped talents. Acquiring education to elevate your earning potential is probably a wise investment. Purging Pluto's crunchy quincunx to this multifaceted Sun-Moon conjunction is a reminder to focus on one subject at a time.

KEEP IN MIND THIS MONTH

A flexible mind reduces friction and opens the door to possibilities that are easy to miss when you stubbornly insist on being right.

KEY DATES

★ **MAY 2**

insatiable hunger

A heart-wrenching Venus-Pluto square can drive you to the depths of your feelings. Disappointment may spew out dramatically, but connecting to your core desires also helps you reach a new level of intimacy. Letting go of someone or something you want is difficult, but well worth it if it leads you to the closeness you crave.

★ **MAY 11–12**

spunky speech

Feisty Mars tangles with Saturn in an awkward quincunx on **May 11** and a scrappy semisquare with Mercury on **May 12**. The warrior planet wants to rush ahead in impulsive Aries, yet the constraints of his passage through your 12th House of Endings may test your patience. Argumentative individuals give you easy targets for your frustration—but unless you enjoy fighting, it's probably a waste of time. Speak clearly and simply to reduce complications, and avoid roundabout conversations that lead you nowhere you want to go.

★ **MAY 14–15**
pleasure without limits
Vivacious Venus puts you in a spending mood with a semisquare to extravagant Jupiter on **May 14**. Dreams of luxury and romance may cause you to overestimate the value of someone or something. Venus forms the same unstable aspect with idealistic Neptune on **May 15** to continue this impractical theme. Still, a greater vision of love, creativity, and pleasure can lift your spirits and stir your imagination. Fantasies of a more rewarding future motivate you to work harder for a bigger payoff down the road.

SUPER NOVA DAYS

★ **MAY 20–23**
idealism and achievement
Venus runs into a bruising quincunx with Saturn on **May 20** that can put the brakes on fun as you are blocked by overly conservative authority figures. Happily, the Sun's entry into

lighthearted Gemini and Mercury's optimistic square with Jupiter provide distraction that quickly overcomes disappointment. Intellectual Mercury's savvy sextile with innovative Uranus on **May 21** reveals shortcut solutions to unresolved issues that are brilliant in their simplicity. Self-conscious Venus in Aries makes a tough semisquare with the Sun on **May 22** that can exaggerate your insecurities, but could also provide a more objective view of your assets. Wise and generous Jupiter joins Chiron in your 10th House of Career on **May 23**, blessing you with a way to combine idealism and material success.

★ **MAY 31**
yours for the taking
Macho Mars enters your sign to fire you up with energy and enthusiasm for the next six weeks. Use this power to advance your interests rather than wasting it in a defensive mode. This is your time to take the lead—but don't forget that practicality and patience will produce tangible results.

JUNE

SWEET TALK

This month bursts with special sweetness as lovely Venus, your ruling planet, enters sensual Taurus on **June 6**. Her annual visit to your sign enhances your capacity for pleasure and casts you in a more attractive light. Take the time to enjoy the delights available to you now. The Full Moon in outgoing Sagittarius on **June 7** falls in your 8th House of Intimacy, which can encourage boldness in your personal life. Stern Saturn, however, forms a tense square to this Sun-Moon opposition, penalizing risky behavior. Stretching your boundaries and speaking the truth are powerful ways to widen the road to love, but carefully choose the time and place for your revelations so that others feel safe enough to truly hear what you have to say. On **June 13**, chatty Mercury zips into its airy home sign of Gemini, where it starts spilling fresh ideas into your 2nd House of Money and Resources. New insights for earning money arise easily but require focus and long-term commitment to turn concept into reality.

Giant Jupiter stops its forward motion and turns retrograde on **June 15**, beginning four months of backpedaling in your 10th House of Career. This doesn't have to block professional advancement, but tells you to assimilate any gains and new duties slowly before you forge ahead. Handling what you already have on your plate is the best way to make a positive impression. The Sun enters Cancer in your 3rd House of Communication on **June 21**, marking the Summer Solstice and warming you up for more personal conversations that draw you closer to others. The protective Cancer New Moon on **June 22** opposes transformational Pluto, stirring deep feelings that could alter your long-range plans.

KEEP IN MIND THIS MONTH

Putting pleasure first is not self-indulgent now; it's the best way to nourish yourself and raise your abilities to their highest potential.

KEY DATES

★ **JUNE 2**
touched by angels

Beautiful Venus brings a bit of heaven down to earth with her harmonious sextiles to the close conjunction of Jupiter, Neptune, and Chiron. The high ideals of this three-planet cluster come alive with spontaneous intuitive insights, instant spiritual connections, inspired art, and the gift of immediate gratification. You sense that everything you want and need is already present, bringing joy to even the most ordinary tasks and elevating your routine to rapture.

SUPER NOVA DAYS

★ **JUNE 6–8**
testing relationships

Venus's entry into Taurus should begin a period of ease and grace, but strict Saturn has some tests for you to pass before letting you climb aboard the gravy train. This hard-nosed planet forms a challenging sesquisquare to Venus on **June 6**, indicating self-doubt and

delays before pleasure is served. Its purpose is
to help you define your worth and be clear
about what you expect from others. The Full
Moon on **June 7** is square Saturn, continuing
the demand for clarity in relationships. Venus's
square to the Moon's Nodes also reflects a
need to alter the ways you connect with others
if you are not being true to yourself. A potent
trine between Venus and regenerative Pluto on
June 8, however, helps you cut past superficial
issues and get to the heart of the matter,
offering satisfaction that may have seemed out
of reach before.

★ **JUNE 16–17**
shifting terrain
Surprises and secrets may shake your confidence in others with an erratic Mars-Uranus
semisquare and a grumpy Mercury-Pluto
quincunx on **June 16**. The expressive Sun's
creative trines with Neptune and Jupiter on
June 17 provide inspiration for happier days.
Patience may be lacking, though, as the Sun
squares and Venus semisquares volatile
Uranus, bringing personal issues to a boil.

Avoid impulsive actions unless they provide brilliant solutions or real breakthroughs that excite you with a newfound sense of freedom.

★ **JUNE 21–23**
push and pull
Romantic Venus conjoins with passionate Mars on **June 21** while also forming a stressful semisquare with the Sun. You can expect a playful and seductive mood, although your insecurity can make anything less than total acceptance feel like rejection. Fortunately, a stabilizing trine between Venus and Saturn on **June 22** helps you create balance and reason to counter emotional extremes. A constructive Mars-Saturn trine the same day exhibits your competence, reliability, and leadership potential. Yet crunchy sesquisquares from Venus and Mars to dark Pluto on **June 23** can evoke jealousy and undermine trust. Seek an opportunity for a private heart-to-heart conversation to work through differences before they get out of hand.

JULY

EXPLORATION AND EXPERIMENTATION

Eclipses often mark unexpected changes, but the two this month appear to be well mannered and easily managed. A **July 7** Lunar Eclipse in businesslike Capricorn and your 9th House of Big Ideas could put a crimp on plans for travel or education. However, solid Saturn forms a stabilizing trine to the Moon, giving you a handle on the situation, even if you're in unfamiliar territory. Then a Solar Eclipse in sensitive Cancer on **July 21** touches your 3rd House of Information. This would normally scramble messages or complicate details, but innovative Uranus forms a trine to the Sun-Moon conjunction, spurring intuitive answers to resolve problems in unexpected ways. Discussing delicate personal matters may prove less difficult than you anticipate, freeing you to be more emotionally honest and vulnerable.

Intellectual Mercury's shift into watery Cancer on **July 3** adds feeling to every thought and conversation, yet Venus and Mars move into airy Gemini on **July 5 and July 11** to favor playfulness and flexibility. While you may display a more flirtatious attitude, you're probably not as carefree as you seem. Mentally, you are mindful to stay within safe boundaries even as you taste different experiences and explore novel styles of expression, opening you to new people and pleasures. Joyful Jupiter joins compassionate Neptune on **July 10** and healing Chiron on **July 22** to reinvigorate imagination and faith in the second of a series of conjunctions that began in late May and finishes in December. Their union in idealistic Aquarius expands your professional horizons with a sense of higher purpose, motivating you to make a more meaningful contribution to society.

KEEP IN MIND THIS MONTH

Experimenting with different ways to work, play, and love is not a sign of uncertainty, but one of self-confidence and trust.

KEY DATES

SUPER NOVA DAYS

★ **JULY 1–2**
in the lap of luxury
Venus makes a stressful square with imaginative Neptune on **July 1** that clouds your judgment. Avoid self-sacrifice for love's sake, and beware careless purchases that don't offer a fair return on your investment. Mercury's trines to Jupiter and Neptune make for inspiring conversation, but a sudden breakdown in communication is possible as erratic Uranus also squares the messenger planet. The square on **July 2** between pleasure-loving Venus and abundant Jupiter can lead you to indulge or overestimate yourself. Fortunately, an insightful Venus-Uranus sextile gives you more intelligent paths to pleasure.

★ **JULY 6–7**
chasing rainbows
Avoid overcommitting yourself right now, especially at work. With assertive Mars squaring squishy Neptune and extravagant Jupiter on

July 6, chasing illusions or stretching yourself too far can undermine your credibility. Venus's quincunx with Pluto the same day reminds you to be selective in your personal and professional choices. You can't satisfy everyone at the same time, so make your priorities clear. The strategic Capricorn Full Moon Eclipse on **July 7** helps you let go of old ambitions that don't correspond with your current needs, while a Mars-Uranus sextile can connect you with a clever colleague to produce original work.

★ **JULY 14–16**
verbal dodgeball
A clunky quincunx between Mars and Pluto on **July 14** brings unfinished business to the surface. Whether you are the target or want to vent your own feelings, it takes a cool head to keep emotions from becoming destructive. Mercury and Jupiter also form a quincunx on **July 15**, fomenting exaggeration that complicates communication. Happily, common sense arrives on **July 16** with the Moon in Taurus and a brilliant Mercury-Uranus trine to spark your intuition. Still, Mercury's tense semisquare to

Venus suggests that personal opinions tend to
touch soft spots, so be gentle when sending
and sterner when receiving.

★ **JULY 21–22**
the price of love
A tough Venus-Saturn square on **July 21** tests
both your relationships and your self-worth,
but you will gain much more than you lose if
it forces you to be more specific about your
desires and values. The Sun's entry into
expressive Leo and conjunction with the karmic
Lunar South Node on **July 22** may provoke a
family drama, yet events also arouse your inner
child and warm your heart with playfulness.

★ **JULY 27–28**
boundless joy
Venus trines lucky Jupiter on **July 27** and
Neptune on **July 28**, expanding feelings of
hope and faith and enriching relationship and
financial prospects. However, a square from
Venus to Uranus on the **28th** requires flexibility
if you are to adapt to change and turn an unexpected problem to a source of pleasure.

AUGUST

OPEN YOUR HEART

Venus entered protective Cancer on **July 31** and opposes passionate Pluto on **August 1** to get the month off to an emotionally charged start. Fortunately, mental Mercury enters its earthy home sign, Virgo, on **August 2** to balance strong feelings with rational thinking. This combination is ideal for discussing delicate issues, especially about love and money. The Full Moon in futuristic Aquarius on **August 5** is a Lunar Eclipse falling in your 10th House of Career, placing the relationship between home and work on the front burner. If your public responsibilities leave little time for a personal life, you're likely to feel the stress now. Mars, the action planet in adaptable Gemini, is trine the Full Moon, however, suggesting alternative methods to meet your obligations that help you avoid a crisis.

You're hard-pressed to resist overexpansion when Mars trines Jupiter on **August 13** and the Sun opposes Jupiter on **August 14**. Such enthusiasm is admirable, but the sense of enterprise and adventure you feel works best when you apply it slowly over time, rather than all at once. Binge shopping, eating, exercising, and romance can be fun but are likely to leave you dissatisfied in the end. The New Moon in generous Leo on **August 20** lights up your 4th House of Home and Family to bring joy, drama, and creative impulses to your household. Its oppositions to expansive Jupiter, compassionate Chiron, and imaginative Neptune enrich your personal life with greater spiritual awareness and inspire your professional life with a more fulfilling sense of purpose. Muscular Mars supports this Sun-Moon conjunction with an energetic sextile to turn great ideas into positive action.

KEEP IN MIND THIS MONTH

Brightening up your home and enhancing your family life inspire and motivate you to also act more creatively outside the house.

KEY DATES

★ **AUGUST 1–2**
attitude adjustment

An opposition from self-conscious Venus to inscrutable Pluto on **August 1** exposes flaws in relationships and uncertainty in yourself. Talking with a supportive person helps you express your concerns without fear of criticism. Once you expose your feelings, it's time to move on and turn worry into action. Mercury's entry into your 5th House of Romance and Self-Expression on **August 2** is excellent for this purpose. Clear thinking reveals a road map to repairing a broken heart or the means to demonstrate your creative abilities with skillful precision.

★ **AUGUST 9–10**
tender and tough

Venus's sesquisquare to Neptune on **August 9** draws you into tasting a world of fantasy much sweeter than reality can provide. Take inspiration from a magical vision of love, beauty, and delight, but hold on tight to your heart or wallet to avoid an expensive misadventure. Sobering Saturn squares Mars on **August 10**, throwing up barriers of restraint and responsibility that put an end to your illusions. However, if a dream is worthy, this is the day to find the focus and commitment to start working toward its realization.

★ **AUGUST 17–19**
rebel without a cause
A Mercury-Saturn conjunction on **August 17** demands that you pay attention to details, but a fuzzy Sun-Neptune opposition can leave you focusing on the wrong issue. Don't confuse effort with efficiency when a wobbly Mercury-Jupiter quincunx casts bread crumbs on a false trail. Intuition may work better than facts, as a Mars-Neptune trine guides you accurately if you follow your instincts. Electric Uranus throws off sparks with a square to Mars and quincunx to the Sun on **August 18**, provoking a sudden outburst of anger or an urge to rebel. Free yourself to try new tech-niques and explore unconventional methods. Venus forms a constructive sextile with mature

Saturn and a shaky quincunx with Jupiter on
August 19 that contrasts steady values and
common sense with a tendency toward excess.

SUPER NOVA DAYS

★ **AUGUST 26–28**
decision time
Venus conjuncts the karmic Lunar South Node
before roaring into rowdy Leo on **August 26**,
creating a perfect storm for relationship
drama when unfinished business from the
past clashes with your need for affection and
recognition right now. A powerful Mars-Pluto
opposition increases the potential for conflict
due to unwillingness to compromise. Yet if
you can stick to the core issue, you have the
strength to overcome almost any obstacle. The
key question is whether to hold on to someone
or something that no longer satisfies you. A
Venus-Pluto quincunx on **August 27** increases
pressure but finally, on **August 28**, Mercury
comes to the rescue, providing much-needed
perspective and the ability to discuss delicate
matters with intelligence and grace.

SEPTEMBER

POLISH YOUR ACT

Advancing your romantic skills and creative abilities is on the agenda this month with planets lighting up your 5th House of Self-Expression. The courageous Sun's presence through **September 22** is ideal for taking calculated risks that reveal both your feelings and your talent. Your key planet, Venus, enters this house on **September 20** to further encourage your playful side and refine your capacity to attract others with charm and grace. The emotional Pisces Full Moon in your social 11th House on **September 4** contrasts responsibilities to friends and groups with your own personal interests, but could also inspire you to participate in an humanitarian or political cause. Communicative Mercury turns retrograde in your 6th House of Work and Service on **September 7** and will remain in reverse until **September 29**. Complications on the job require more concentration and time at work, while revising your exercise and diet is recommended to ensure good health.

Strict Saturn makes its third opposition to independent Uranus on **September 15**, upping the tension between your need for control and the rebellious behavior of others. The fussy Virgo New Moon on **September 18** can make your desire for order even stronger, yet its conjunction with Saturn and opposition to Uranus demand compromise. Any attempt to dominate will spur strong reactions; respect everyone's free will to maintain a reasonable degree of harmony. The Sun's entry into fair-minded Libra on **September 22** marks the Autumnal Equinox, enabling you to overcome extreme positions and reach the common ground where you can work well with others. Still, the Sun's square with intense Pluto and Mercury's high-frequency opposition to Uranus on **September 23** could put reason on the sidelines as buried feelings explode in strong words and rash actions.

KEEP IN MIND THIS MONTH

Progress, rather than perfection, should be your measure of success now, for even baby steps will advance your interests.

KEY DATES

★ **SEPTEMBER 2–4**
sweet anticipation
Your confidence dips when Venus forms a
semisquare with stifling Saturn on **September 2**.
You can overcome a feeling of being under-
appreciated with some discipline and patience
that will earn you respect. A tight Mercury-
Mars square on **September 3** triggers fast
thinking and snappy comments that can rile
sensitive co-workers. With an itchy Venus-
Uranus semisquare on **September 4**, avoid a
rush to judgment; a more open-minded
approach may take you to unexpected delights.

★ **SEPTEMBER 11–12**
the road of excess
An expansive Venus-Jupiter opposition on
September 11 can put you in the mood to love
excessively and spend lavishly. Enjoy some
self-indulgence, but don't completely lose
touch with reality. An irritating semisquare
between retrograde Mercury and Venus on
September 12 awakens unfinished relationship

issues. Reviewing the past is helpful as long as it provides a healthy perspective that keeps you from repeating the same old story.

SUPER NOVA DAYS

★ **SEPTEMBER 15–17**
rider on the storm

The deep divide between duty and freedom revealed by a Saturn-Uranus opposition on **September 15** comes at a very sensitive time, with Venus opposite Neptune. This idealistic but vulnerable connection makes for tender feelings better suited to romance and spirituality than confrontation. You may want to run away from the harsh realities of the present, and certainly can benefit from some time to relax. However, a failure to address serious issues now may prove costly later. An unsettled Venus-Uranus quincunx on **September 16** feeds frustration and can give you even more reason to flee. Yet if you are willing to let go of fixed expectations and rigid values, you might discover unexpected pleasure or a surprising solution. **September 17** looks like a day of extremes with the Sun opposing Uranus and joining Saturn. A menacing Mercury-Pluto square can undermine trust and trigger power struggles, but the messenger planet then backs into logical Virgo, bringing you the tools to untangle a knotty situation.

★ **SEPTEMBER 20–21**
constant gardener
Venus enters earthy Virgo on **September 20**, helping you create a garden of joy. You can make beauty bloom like flowers in the desert and bring happiness to those nearby. Venus also forms a productive trine with resourceful Pluto, which empowers you to transform awkward moments into pleasant ones and extract what you need under almost any conditions. This harmonious aspect deepens relationships with controlled passion that produces lasting delight. Connections with others may be less smooth on **September 21** when aggressive Mars rubs against Venus in an irritating semi-square. However, the forces of Eros are rising to turn an ordinary day into a sassy and sensual time.

OCTOBER

ON-THE-JOB TRAINING

The process of redefining your professional life begins this month as successful Jupiter goes direct in your 10th House of Career on **October 12**. This vocational emphasis is reinforced when disciplined Saturn enters your 6th House of Work and Service on **October 29**. Jupiter expands your vision and increases opportunities for greater recognition and more fulfilling responsibilities. Saturn suggests that additional training may be required to achieve these potentials. Several planets in relationship-oriented air signs underscore your ability to work with others as a critical element to reaching your goals. The impatient Aries Full Moon on **October 4**, however, stirs hidden desires—perhaps even an urge to run away from it all. This is a reminder of how important it is to take breaks from the stresses of daily life. A relaxing hobby, physical activity, or spiritual pursuit with no connection to your job is a not a waste of time, but an essential factor in maintaining good health and productivity.

Domestic challenges are possible when assertive Mars enters brash Leo and your 4th

House of Home and Family on **October 16**, followed by a testy quincunx with Pluto on **October 18**. You can turn dramatic emotions in a constructive direction by clearing out unneeded objects and outdated attitudes that stand in the way of making your living space more reflective of your highest values. The gracious Libra New Moon, also on **October 18**, forms a forgiving trine with sympathetic Neptune, helping you release past grievances and become more open to cooperative alliances on the job. Your feelings of insecurity, or those of your co-workers, can be significantly reduced if you step back and take a strategic approach rather than allowing your immediate impulses to rule.

KEEP IN MIND THIS MONTH

Your support and loyalty to others build a reserve of goodwill that is well worth the sacrifice of your time.

KEY DATES

★ **OCTOBER 4**
reckless fun
Electric Uranus is giving you an itch for excitement with its opposition to mental Mercury and trine to active Mars. Fast thinking and unconventional experiences can bring thrills you don't usually seek. But measure the costs, because your values may be skewed by an overly optimistic Venus-Jupiter quincunx and your physical judgment blurred with Mars forming the same unstable angle with illusory Neptune.

★ **OCTOBER 8–9**
watch your step
A strict Mercury-Saturn conjunction on **October 8** is excellent for making a clear statement as long as it's all fact and no fluff. If you are uncertain about specific details, hold your tongue until you find the right answer. Sensible Venus in Virgo drops the usual social and financial rules on **October 9** with her opposition to shocking Uranus and a quincunx

with dreamy Neptune. Despite new sources of delight, restlessness can shake a relationship or lead to a questionable purchase.

SUPER NOVA DAYS

★ **OCTOBER 13–15**
rise to the challenge
A restraining conjunction between Venus and Saturn on **October 13** can put you in a serious mood. The purpose, though, is not to eliminate pleasure but to make you clarify what you want and what you're willing to do to get it. Don't complain if you feel undervalued; instead, commit to developing your talents to their full potential. Venus enters artful Libra and your 6th House of Skills on **October 14**, bringing grace to the workplace, along with ideas for polishing your creative gifts. However, a square between Venus and intense Pluto on **October 15** challenges you to dig deeply within yourself to find what you need. Relationship resentment is possible, but it's only a problem if you refuse to make any changes.

★ **OCTOBER 23–24**
relationship repair

The Sun enters passionate Scorpio on
October 23 and sextiles intense Pluto on the
24th. The healthy alignment of this powerful
pair deepens relationships, helping you deal
with touchy subjects more effectively to regain
trust and restore self-confidence.

★ **OCTOBER 28–29**
play nice

Be sociable on **October 28** as chatty Mercury
enters your 7th House of Relationships while
Venus forms a sweet trine with upbeat Jupiter.
Make time for a little midweek partying or a
shopping spree with friends to celebrate. On
the other hand, a tense Sun-Mars square on
October 29 can incite conflict with a control-
ling person. Avoid locking down in a battle of
wills that can wear you out. Use the pressure
you feel to push yourself ahead instead of trying to push someone else out of the way.

NOVEMBER

FRESH PERSPECTIVES

The Full Moon in stubborn Taurus on **November 2** is square assertive Mars, stirring up relationship conflicts and perhaps even anger with yourself. Channel the powerful energy you feel in a positive direction with healthy physical activity or by starting a new project. Balancing force with finesse will help keep the peace and allow you to sustain a long-term effort by avoiding obstacles instead of battling them. Idealistic Neptune's direct turn in your 10th House of Career on **November 4** awakens dreams of more inspiring work that could turn an ordinary job into a meaningful contribution to society. Your ruling planet, Venus, enters emotionally deep Scorpio and your 7th House of Partnerships on **November 7**, which is bound to intensify relationships. The stakes in the game of love are getting higher as your desire for more may upset a current companion or attract the ardor of a new one.

On **November 15**, planetary heavyweights Saturn and Pluto make the first of three stressful squares that agitate the work-related houses in your chart. Difficulty with authorities on the job or increased pressure with reduced rewards may force you to consider a major change by the time this pattern finishes next August. The New Moon in magnetic Scorpio on **November 16** increases your drive to deepen your connections with others. A creative trine with unusual Uranus reveals surprising ways to bring excitement to your relationships, but a stressful square to imprecise Neptune could lead you to disappointment if fantasy overcomes common sense. The Sun's entry into adventurous Sagittarius and your 8th House of Intimacy on **November 21** encourages risk taking and generosity; these can be the keys toward empowering your emotional and financial alliances.

KEEP IN MIND THIS MONTH

Letting go of what you already have may not be easy, but it frees you to receive even more in return.

KEY DATES

★ **NOVEMBER 2–3**
a wild ride
Intellectual Mercury, sociable Venus, and
assertive Mars all form tense aspects with
eccentric Uranus on **November 2**. Brilliant
ideas and spontaneous fun are positive potentials, yet require faith and a good deal of flexibility. If you insist on resisting change, expect
an unsettled day of less-than-pleasant surprises. Happily, a Venus-Neptune trine reveals
potential for confidence in people and things
that you don't fully understand. Venus squares
the Moon's Nodes on **November 3**, which can
make you more sensitive to how people react
to you. If you're not receiving the love or
respect you believe you deserve, think carefully
before making an issue of it.

SUPER NOVA DAYS

★ **NOVEMBER 7–9**
your heart's desire
Venus's entry into Scorpio on **November 7**
offers richness in relationships, but may

require some complex negotiations. A Mercury-Pluto semisquare takes conversations below the surface to address underlying issues that you might prefer to avoid. It's healthier to engage your concerns than to deny them. The Sun in your 7th House of Partnerships forms tense semisquares with Saturn and Pluto on **November 8** that may attract jealousy, delay gratification, and cause you to measure your moves very carefully. Information overflow from a Mercury-Jupiter square engenders exaggeration: Cut what you hear in half for a more accurate assessment. Lovely Venus sextiles regenerative Pluto on **November 9**, bringing you to the heart of love and value. Your radar for connecting with the essence of yourself and others accurately guides you to obtain what you desire at the best possible price.

★ **NOVEMBER 19–21**
long-term commitment
Venus bounces from a square to Mars on **November 19** to semisquares with Saturn and Pluto on **November 21** that first excite you,

incite you, and then slow you down. Venus-Mars leads to sparring that can be erotic when it's playful or destructive when it's not. The love planet's hard angles to Saturn and Pluto may stir resentment, mistrust, and doubt. Yet reason brings clarity and the resolve needed to define limits and set clear goals that can be achieved with patience and dedication.

★ **NOVEMBER 25–26**
nothing to prove
A creative Venus-Uranus trine on **November 25** opens your taste buds to new and different experiences that could unlock a sticky relationship or financial situation. Allow your imagination free rein, since unconventional thinking spurs possibilities ordinary logic would never find. A Venus-Neptune square on **November 26** increases your sensitivity to others' opinions. If you are feeling vulnerable, avoid trying to prove yourself; take shelter in spirituality, romance, and fantasy instead.

DECEMBER

GROWING PAINS

Three lunations (New and Full Moons), three planets changing direction, and two outer planet conjunctions create a very busy month. Revolutionary Uranus turns forward on **December 1** in your 11th House of Groups, sparking original approaches to teamwork. Venus enters Sagittarius and your 8th House of Intimacy the same day to provoke a more adventurous spirit in emotional and financial matters. The Full Moon in mutable Gemini on **December 2** tickles your 2nd House of Income, stimulating new ideas about making money, while a helpful trine from practical Saturn provides patience and a manageable plan. Hopeful Jupiter joins wounded Chiron on **December 7**, enriching painful experiences with meaning that can hasten healing. The enthusiastic Sagittarius New Moon on **December 16** is supported by sextiles from Jupiter, Neptune, and Chiron to empower your dreams and fulfill your material and spiritual needs.

Macho Mars turns retrograde in your 4th House of Roots on **December 20**, perhaps forcing you to step back and deal with unfinished business at home before advancing professionally. Generosity and faith bless your holiday season when Jupiter joins spiritual Neptune on the Winter Solstice, **December 21**. Venus enters your 9th House of Travel and Higher Education on **December 25**, gifting you with a desire to expand your horizons. However, chatty Mercury turns retrograde on **December 26**, retracing its steps in this house so you can reevaluate your beliefs and reconsider educational or travel-related plans. A Lunar Eclipse in moody Cancer on **December 31** ends the year on a somber note as Saturn squares and Venus and Pluto oppose the Full Moon. Emotionally intense conversations can feel threatening, but facing the truth is hard work that rewards you with greater trust and respect.

KEEP IN MIND THIS MONTH

Taken with care and thought—not fear—a step backward can be more courageous than blindly forging ahead.

KEY DATES

★ **DECEMBER 4–5**
stay in control
A smart sextile between value-based Venus
and thrifty Saturn on **December 4** helps you
make wise shopping decisions. Your good
sense shines through in relationships, too,
allowing you to maintain a clear and solid
presence in an emotionally charged situation.
On **December 5**, Mercury enters pragmatic
Capricorn and impulsive Mars is slowed by a
semisquare to Saturn, thwarting spontaneity;
avoid changing plans at the last minute.
Organizing your time carefully, however,
produces desirable results.

★ **DECEMBER 9**
surprising answers
You can work your way out of tricky situations
as your planet, Venus, forms clever quintiles
with Jupiter and Chiron. If you are stressed
by a conflict between professional obligations
and personal needs, this creative 72-degree
alignment reveals unconventional solutions.

★ **DECEMBER 17**
friendly frolic

A sassy Venus-Mars trine puts you in the
mood to play and could attract someone
special to share the fun. Creative activities,
games, and flirting come easily to you now;
even when you mean well, however, you could
hit a sore spot with a highly sensitive person.
The issues feel totally real to this individual, so
respect his or her reactions without becoming
defensive about what you've said or done.

SUPER NOVA DAYS

★ **DECEMBER 19–21**
make it happen

An excitable Venus-Uranus square on
December 19 brings more surprises than stability. Quick changes in tastes and opinions
may rattle your sense of safety, especially in
relationships. Yet if you can keep an open
mind, discovering new sources of delight
makes any inconvenience worth the price.
Venus forms supportive sextiles to buoyant
Jupiter late on **December 20** and to Neptune
early on **December 21**—fortunate alignments

that lift your spirits and carry you through any emotional storm. Jupiter and Neptune's precise conjunction, along with the Sun's entry into ambitious Capricorn, make this a rare occasion when your highest ideals and aspirations are matched with the will and the plan to make them real.

★ **DECEMBER 28–29**
take a stand
The air thickens with deep feelings as Venus joins Pluto and sesquisquares Mars on **December 28**. Resentment, mistrust, and jealousy are possible, yet discomfort can force you to expose your fears and clarify your desires. Venus's square to karmic Saturn on **December 29** is a time to draw a line in the sand regarding relationships and self-worth issues. Be prepared to simply say no or to state your position without equivocation. Respect is more important than approval now, so stand up for what you know is right.

APPENDIXES

★

2009 MONTH-AT-A-GLANCE ASTROCALENDAR

★

FAMOUS TAUREANS

★

TAURUS IN LOVE

THURSDAY 1

FRIDAY 2

SATURDAY 3 ★ Use the power of gentle persuasion to motivate others

SUNDAY 4 ★

MONDAY 5

TUESDAY 6

WEDNESDAY 7

THURSDAY 8

FRIDAY 9 ★ Experiment with approaches before finding the right formula

SATURDAY 10 ★

SUNDAY 11 ★

MONDAY 12

TUESDAY 13

WEDNESDAY 14

THURSDAY 15

FRIDAY 16

SATURDAY 17 ★ Brilliant but erratic describes your mental state on the 18th

SUNDAY 18 ★

MONDAY 19

TUESDAY 20

WEDNESDAY 21

THURSDAY 22 ★ SUPER NOVA DAYS Handle complicated personal business
with courage and maturity

FRIDAY 23 ★

SATURDAY 24 ★

SUNDAY 25

MONDAY 26

TUESDAY 27

WEDNESDAY 28

THURSDAY 29

FRIDAY 30

SATURDAY 31

SUNDAY 1

MONDAY 2 ★ Decision-making may not be at its best

TUESDAY 3

WEDNESDAY 4 ★ Discuss your differences rather than suffer in silence

THURSDAY 5 ★

FRIDAY 6

SATURDAY 7

SUNDAY 8

MONDAY 9

TUESDAY 10

WEDNESDAY 11 ★ Prioritize your responsibilities on the 12th

THURSDAY 12 ★

FRIDAY 13

SATURDAY 14

SUNDAY 15

MONDAY 16 ★ SUPER NOVA DAYS Charm is a powerful force in your personal and professional life

TUESDAY 17 ★

WEDNESDAY 18 ★

THURSDAY 19

FRIDAY 20

SATURDAY 21

SUNDAY 22

MONDAY 23

TUESDAY 24 ★ The 24th sparks bright ideas and scintillating conversations

WEDNESDAY 25 ★

THURSDAY 26

FRIDAY 27

SATURDAY 28

SUNDAY 1

MONDAY 2

TUESDAY 3

WEDNESDAY 4

THURSDAY 5

FRIDAY 6 ★ **SUPER NOVA DAYS** Aim high, but stay grounded

SATURDAY 7 ★

SUNDAY 8 ★

MONDAY 9

TUESDAY 10

WEDNESDAY 11

THURSDAY 12

FRIDAY 13

SATURDAY 14 ★ Deal intelligently with strong feelings

SUNDAY 15

MONDAY 16

TUESDAY 17

WEDNESDAY 18 ★ Cut a big task down to a manageable size

THURSDAY 19 ★

FRIDAY 20

SATURDAY 21

SUNDAY 22 ★ Intellectual impulsiveness proves exciting, but not practical

MONDAY 23

TUESDAY 24

WEDNESDAY 25

THURSDAY 26

FRIDAY 27 ★ Emotions are much stronger than reason now

SATURDAY 28 ★

SUNDAY 29

MONDAY 30

TUESDAY 31

WEDNESDAY 1

THURSDAY 2

FRIDAY 3 ★ Learning what doesn't work precedes meaningful change

SATURDAY 4 *

SUNDAY 5

MONDAY 6

TUESDAY 7

WEDNESDAY 8

THURSDAY 9 ★ Reawaken romantic dreams and connections on the 11th

FRIDAY 10 ★

SATURDAY 11 ★

SUNDAY 12

MONDAY 13

TUESDAY 14

WEDNESDAY 15 ★ Don't stifle change—allow as much movement as possible

THURSDAY 16 ★

FRIDAY 17 ★

SATURDAY 18

SUNDAY 19

MONDAY 20

TUESDAY 21 ★ SUPER NOVA DAYS Explore without justifying your behavior

WEDNESDAY 22 ★

THURSDAY 23 ★

FRIDAY 24 ★

SATURDAY 25

SUNDAY 26 ★ Focus on taking care of business

MONDAY 27

TUESDAY 28

WEDNESDAY 29

THURSDAY 30

FRIDAY 1

SATURDAY 2 ★ Letting go of something you want will lead to closeness

SUNDAY 3

MONDAY 4

TUESDAY 5

WEDNESDAY 6

THURSDAY 7

FRIDAY 8

SATURDAY 9

SUNDAY 10

MONDAY 11 ★ Speak clearly to reduce complications

TUESDAY 12 ★

WEDNESDAY 13

THURSDAY 14 ★ Visions of love, creativity, and pleasure stir your imagination

FRIDAY 15 ★

SATURDAY 16

SUNDAY 17

MONDAY 18

TUESDAY 19

WEDNESDAY 20 ★ SUPER NOVA DAYS Combine idealism and material success

THURSDAY 21 ★

FRIDAY 22 ★

SATURDAY 23 ★

SUNDAY 24

MONDAY 25

TUESDAY 26

WEDNESDAY 27

THURSDAY 28

FRIDAY 29

SATURDAY 30

SUNDAY 31 ★ Practicality and patience produce tangible results

MONDAY 1

TUESDAY 2 ★ Everything you want and need is already present

WEDNESDAY 3

THURSDAY 4

FRIDAY 5

SATURDAY 6 ★ **SUPER NOVA DAYS** Cut away superficial issues—get to the heart of the matter

SUNDAY 7 ★

MONDAY 8 ★

TUESDAY 9

WEDNESDAY 10

THURSDAY 11

FRIDAY 12

SATURDAY 13

SUNDAY 14

MONDAY 15

TUESDAY 16 ★ Unless they provide brilliant solutions, avoid impulsive actions

WEDNESDAY 17 ★

THURSDAY 18

FRIDAY 19

SATURDAY 20

SUNDAY 21 ★ Work through differences on the 23rd

MONDAY 22 ★

TUESDAY 23 ★

WEDNESDAY 24

THURSDAY 25

FRIDAY 26

SATURDAY 27

SUNDAY 28

MONDAY 29

TUESDAY 30

WEDNESDAY 1 ★ **SUPER NOVA DAYS** Avoid self-sacrifice for love's sake

---

THURSDAY 2 ★

FRIDAY 3

SATURDAY 4

SUNDAY 5

MONDAY 6 ★ Let go of old ambitions that don't correlate with current needs

---

TUESDAY 7 ★

WEDNESDAY 8

THURSDAY 9

FRIDAY 10

SATURDAY 11

SUNDAY 12

MONDAY 13

TUESDAY 14 ★ Tread gently—opinions tend to touch soft spots

WEDNESDAY 15 ★

THURSDAY 16 ★

FRIDAY 17

SATURDAY 18

SUNDAY 19

MONDAY 20

TUESDAY 21 ★ You'll gain more if you're specific about your desires

---

WEDNESDAY 22 ★

THURSDAY 23

FRIDAY 24

SATURDAY 25

SUNDAY 26

MONDAY 27 ★ Turn an unexpected problem into a source of pleasure

---

TUESDAY 28 ★

WEDNESDAY 29

THURSDAY 30

FRIDAY 31

SATURDAY 1 ★ Expose your feelings, turn worry into action

SUNDAY 2 ★

MONDAY 3

TUESDAY 4

WEDNESDAY 5

THURSDAY 6

FRIDAY 7

SATURDAY 8

SUNDAY 9 ★ Take inspiration from a magical vision of love

MONDAY 10 ★

TUESDAY 11

WEDNESDAY 12

THURSDAY 13

FRIDAY 14

SATURDAY 15

SUNDAY 16

MONDAY 17 ★ Pay attention to details on the 17th

TUESDAY 18 ★

WEDNESDAY 19 ★

THURSDAY 20

FRIDAY 21

SATURDAY 22

SUNDAY 23

MONDAY 24

TUESDAY 25

WEDNESDAY 26 ★ **SUPER NOVA DAYS** Discuss delicate matters with intelligence and grace

THURSDAY 27 ★

FRIDAY 28 ★

SATURDAY 29

SUNDAY 30

MONDAY 31

TUESDAY 1

WEDNESDAY 2 ★ Avoid a rush to judgment, take an open-minded approach

THURSDAY 3 ★

FRIDAY 4 ★

SATURDAY 5

SUNDAY 6

MONDAY 7

TUESDAY 8

WEDNESDAY 9

THURSDAY 10

FRIDAY 11 ★ The 12th awakens unfinished relationship issues

SATURDAY 12 ★

SUNDAY 13

MONDAY 14

TUESDAY 15 ★ SUPER NOVA DAYS Let go of rigid expectations and values

WEDNESDAY 16 ★

THURSDAY 17 ★

FRIDAY 18

SATURDAY 19

SUNDAY 20 ★ Relationships deepen with controlled passion

MONDAY 21 ★

TUESDAY 22

WEDNESDAY 23

THURSDAY 24

FRIDAY 25

SATURDAY 26

SUNDAY 27

MONDAY 28

TUESDAY 29

WEDNESDAY 30

THURSDAY 1

FRIDAY 2

SATURDAY 3

SUNDAY 4 ★ Fast thinking and unconventional experiences bring thrills

MONDAY 5

TUESDAY 6

WEDNESDAY 7

THURSDAY 8 ★ The 8th is excellent for making a clear statement

FRIDAY 9 ★

SATURDAY 10

SUNDAY 11

MONDAY 12

TUESDAY 13 ★ SUPER NOVA DAYS Dig deeply to find what you need

WEDNESDAY 14 ★

THURSDAY 15 ★

FRIDAY 16

SATURDAY 17

SUNDAY 18

MONDAY 19

TUESDAY 20

WEDNESDAY 21

THURSDAY 22

FRIDAY 23 ★ Regain trust and restore self-confidence

SATURDAY 24 ★

SUNDAY 25

MONDAY 26

TUESDAY 27

WEDNESDAY 28 ★ Use the pressure you feel to push yourself ahead

THURSDAY 29 ★

FRIDAY 30

SATURDAY 31

SUNDAY 1

MONDAY 2 ★ Brilliant ideas and spontaneous fun are had on the 2nd

TUESDAY 3 ★

WEDNESDAY 4

THURSDAY 5

FRIDAY 6

SATURDAY 7 ★ SUPER NOVA DAYS The 7th offers richness in relationships

SUNDAY 8 ★

MONDAY 9 ★

TUESDAY 10

WEDNESDAY 11

THURSDAY 12

FRIDAY 13

SATURDAY 14

SUNDAY 15

MONDAY 16

TUESDAY 17

WEDNESDAY 18

THURSDAY 19 ★ Clear goals are achieved with patience and dedication

FRIDAY 20 ★

SATURDAY 21 ★

SUNDAY 22

MONDAY 23

TUESDAY 24

WEDNESDAY 25 ★ Take shelter in spirituality, romance, and fantasy

THURSDAY 26 ★

FRIDAY 27

SATURDAY 28

SUNDAY 29

MONDAY 30

TUESDAY 1

WEDNESDAY 2

THURSDAY 3

FRIDAY 4 ★ Organizing your time carefully produces desirable results

SATURDAY 5 ★

SUNDAY 6

MONDAY 7

TUESDAY 8

WEDNESDAY 9 ★ Use unconventional solutions to fix tricky situations

THURSDAY 10

FRIDAY 11

SATURDAY 12

SUNDAY 13

MONDAY 14

TUESDAY 15

WEDNESDAY 16

THURSDAY 17 ★ A playful mood could attract someone special

FRIDAY 18

SATURDAY 19 ★ SUPER NOVA DAYS The 19th brings surprises

SUNDAY 20 ★

MONDAY 21 ★

TUESDAY 22

WEDNESDAY 23

THURSDAY 24

FRIDAY 25

SATURDAY 26

SUNDAY 27

MONDAY 28 ★ The air thickens with deep feelings on the 28th

TUESDAY 29 ★

WEDNESDAY 30

THURSDAY 31

FAMOUS TAUREANS

Jessica Lange	★	4/20/1949
Joan Miró	★	4/20/1893
Queen Elizabeth II	★	4/21/1926
Charlotte Brontë	★	4/21/1816
Catherine the Great	★	4/21/1729
Iggy Pop	★	4/21/1947
Vladimir Ilyich Lenin	★	4/22/1870
Jack Nicholson	★	4/22/1937
William Shakespeare	★	4/23/1564
Shirley Temple Black	★	4/23/1928
Vladimir Nabokov	★	4/23/1899
Lee Majors	★	4/23/1939
Sandra Dee	★	4/23/1942
Michael Moore	★	4/23/1954
Barbra Streisand	★	4/24/1942
Jean-Paul Gaultier	★	4/24/1952
Kelly Clarkson	★	4/24/1982
Shirley MacLaine	★	4/24/1934
Al Pacino	★	4/25/1940
Ella Fitzgerald	★	4/25/1918
Edward R. Murrow	★	4/25/1908
Renee Zellweger	★	4/25/1969
I. M. Pei	★	4/26/1917
Carol Burnett	★	4/26/1933
Samuel Morse	★	4/27/1791
Ulysses S. Grant	★	4/27/1822
Jay Leno	★	4/28/1950
Harper Lee	★	4/28/1926
Ann-Margret	★	4/28/1941
William Randolph Hearst	★	4/29/1863
Duke Ellington	★	4/29/1899
Dale Earnhardt	★	4/29/1951
Jerry Seinfeld	★	4/29/1954
Uma Thurman	★	4/29/1970
Willie Nelson	★	4/30/1933

FAMOUS TAUREANS

Kirsten Dunst	★	4/30/1982
Jack Paar	★	5/1/1918
Dr. Benjamin Spock	★	5/2/1903
David Beckham	★	5/2/1975
Niccolo Machiavelli	★	5/3/1469
Golda Meir	★	5/3/1898
Bing Crosby	★	5/3/1903
James Brown	★	5/3/1933
Audrey Hepburn	★	5/4/1929
Karl Marx	★	5/5/1818
Sigmund Freud	★	5/6/1856
Orson Welles	★	5/6/1915
George Clooney	★	5/6/1961
Robert Browning	★	5/7/1812
Johannes Brahms	★	5/7/1833
Eva Perón	★	5/7/1919
Johnny Unitas	★	5/7/1933
Rick Nelson	★	5/8/1940
Billy Joel	★	5/9/1949
Sid Vicious	★	5/10/1957
Paul "Bono" Hewson	★	5/10/1960
Fred Astaire	★	5/10/1899
Salvador Dalí	★	5/11/1904
Katharine Hepburn	★	5/12/1907
Yogi Berra	★	5/12/1925
Stevie Wonder	★	5/13/1950
Cate Blanchett	★	5/14/1969
Bobby Darin	★	5/14/1936
Madeleine Albright	★	5/15/1937
Liberace	★	5/16/1919
Pierce Brosnan	★	5/16/1953
Janet Jackson	★	5/16/1966
Sugar Ray Leonard	★	5/17/1956
Tina Fey	★	5/18/1970
Malcolm X	★	5/19/1925
Cher	★	5/20/1946

TAURUS IN LOVE

TAURUS–ARIES (MARCH 21–APRIL 19)

You Bulls are the most practical and dependable people in the zodiac and may question the impulsive actions of your Aries partner. You'll want to apply Aries's new and highly creative ideas into practical actions. Aries might resist your steadfast ways— they don't like it when life becomes entrenched in routine. Your excitable partner isn't known for his or her ability to tolerate repetitive tasks, even if they bring you security and comfort. You don't have much patience for your Aries mate's unfinished business or halfhearted commitments. Of course, other planets in your birth chart can change this. For example, if you have Mercury or Venus in Aries, you'll better understand your spontaneous partner. With your Moon in any fire sign (Aries, Leo, or Sagittarius), you'll have increased chances for a successful union. The true test lies in your ability to remain open to the Ram's impractical enthusiasm without feeling responsible to bring him or her to their senses. Allow room for change and there'll be plenty of desire and lust between you two that can last a very long time.

TAURUS–TAURUS (APRIL 20–MAY 20)

You are stubborn, loyal, earthy, and patient. Often you are slow to change, preferring the solid and familiar. When meeting a fellow Bull for romance, there will be a practical approach to love and marriage. Both of you possess steadfast values and a well-defined picture of the world around you. Relationships are rarely tolerable for you if you feel out of sync with your partner's value system. As long as you and your Taurus partner have similar philosophies about love, family, and money, the prerequisites for a deep bond are present. The two of you can both enjoy activities such as gardening, hiking, or having a picnic. You are both willing to satiate your senses and probably share a love of eating; remain vigilant about encouraging each other toward laziness and watch each other's carb intake. Starting projects together may be difficult, but once started, you'll see them through. Taureans can be quite different depending on the placement of the other planets in their birth charts. If your Moon is in a fire sign (Aries, Leo, or Sagittarius) or air sign (Gemini, Libra, or Aquarius), your differences can feel stressful. Yet you can both be quite happy as you move relentlessly toward creating your life together.

TAURUS–GEMINI (MAY 21–JUNE 20)

Your sign is ruled by Venus, the planet of love and beauty, connecting you to your senses. Taurus folks often have pleasant voices and yet you say what you mean. Your Gemini partner is ruled by Mercury, the messenger planet, which is associated with breath, the spoken word, and all forms of language. Together, you two can find immense pleasure in sharing the arts, and may enchant each other with your different styles of creative expertise. You're more attracted to sensual creativity, such as music, massage, and art forms that impact both sight and touch. Your Gemini partner may gravitate more toward poetry, riddles, and lighthearted play. Both of you enjoy nature, and would most likely enjoy the splendor of parks and outdoor theater. This relationship is easier if you were born with the Moon or Mars in an air sign. Otherwise, you may find that your Gemini lover is too flighty and changeable for your tastes. On the other hand, this relationship can bring movement and excitement into your life. In fact, this can be a nice match up if you are willing to stretch yourself beyond your physical comfort zones and move into the Gemini's mental world of words and ideas.

TAURUS–CANCER (JUNE 21–JULY 22)

When you are comfortable, you are very easy to be around. And with Cancer the Crab, you can find a natural comfort zone which can lull you into an easy relaxation. You're drawn toward the domestic behaviors of Cancer and can be the happy recipient of their cooking, homemaking, and nurturing, whether they are male or female. In fact, since you like to treat your senses well, the two of you living together would most likely create a magnificent kitchen and a comfortable living space. The culinary delights that might come from your kitchen are viewed as caring and nurturing by your Cancer partner, but you simply love to eat what is prepared, no matter what the motivation is for preparing it. You are willing and capable to provide a steady and stable foundation for the security-bound Cancer, and they, in turn, happily offer you a safe comfortable haven. Your lover may seem emotionally needy, unless your Moon or Mars is in a water sign (Cancer, Scorpio, or Pisces). There is a high degree of trust that exists between you two, and if you establish harmony early in your relationship, you can remain together for a lifetime.

TAURUS–LEO (JULY 23–AUGUST 22)

You and your Leo partner are two of the four "fixed signs" of the zodiac, meaning you are less yielding and more stubborn than other astrological sun signs. There can be trouble because of this factor, especially when you and your Leo partner clash over how best to get your personal needs met and your individual styles of expressing love. You can be possessive and bull-headed and your lover can become jealous and needy. You both have simplistic childlike tendencies that can prove to be detrimental. You must aim high together to overcome the petty fears and emotions that can overwhelm the trust and love you have for each other. You have to learn how to take turns being flexible. At times, you may get frustrated by your partner's self-centeredness, but if you tolerate his or her different style, you can be highly physical and quite romantic together. If you have Venus in Aries or the Moon in any fire sign (Aries, Leo, or Sagittarius), this can sufficiently ease potential conflicts. Ultimately, the key is in learning early on how to sustain an enduring attitude of love and respect for your Lion. If you can do this, the two of you can endure hardships, share fun, and take on the world with zest and determination.

TAURUS–VIRGO (AUGUST 23–SEPT. 22)

You earthy Bulls function quite differently than Virgos—another earth sign—yet you remain quite compatible as you share a practical approach to life. Your Virgo lover is ruled by the mental planet Mercury, is fixated on details and perfection, and edits life with a fine-tooth comb. His or her analytical and sometimes critical style can put you into a tailspin. You're probably more grounded, and opt to make your basic decisions by simplification and determination rather than complex analysis. Your planet, Venus, is more focused on the practical realities of love, the physical pleasures it can offer, and plain old good-hearted fun. With a Virgo, you can unite intellect with emotion. You make a good team because you bridge the head and heart in a practical and tangible way by sharing similar interests and concerns. If the Moon or Mars in your chart is in Gemini or Sagittarius, there can be stressful differences of lifestyle, making compatibility more difficult. Whatever stresses other planetary placements may add, good team-work and mutual respect makes this a feel-good combination that can stand up to the test of time.

TAURUS–LIBRA (SEPT. 23–OCT. 22)

Both of these zodiacal signs are associated with
the planet Venus, creating a mutual desire for
love, beauty, and refined communication. You are
an earth sign, however, and tend to be more
sensual through body, emotion, and physical
desire. You need to bring things down to the
sensory level for them to have the most meaning.
A Libra, however, is an air sign, so your partner
will be mentally intrigued with the idea of love
and harmony. In fact, Libra is a gracious host or
hostess and will like to do things that make you
feel good. A problem could exist between your
strong desire for basic physical pleasure while
your Libra lover reads, draws, and talks about it.
If, on the other hand, you have the Moon in any
air sign (Gemini, Libra, or Aquarius) or if you have
Mercury or Venus in Gemini, these differences can
be minimized and compatibility is increased. The
bottom line is you can find success by drawing up
a plan of strategy and applying it to the practical
aspects of your life. Your home will be comfortable
and is likely to be filled with lots of art, books,
music, and beautiful things.

TAURUS-SCORPIO (OCT. 23-NOV. 21)

You are practical, levelheaded, and more overt with your emotions and needs than the quiet and sometimes moody Scorpio. Both of you are fixed signs and can be stubborn, tending to brood when you cannot have your way. You are less likely to hold a grudge or exhibit silent resentment than your Scorpion lover. Instead, you may try to push your way into his or her psyche. Your determination, however, won't wear down the powerful feelings of your partner. You tend to be simplistic in your physical needs, while Scorpio's sensuality and sexuality are more complicated than you can imagine. As opposite signs of the zodiac, you are attracted to each other and can be extremely sexy together. If the placement of other planets in your chart—especially the Moon or Mars—is in any water sign (Cancer, Scorpio, or Pisces), then you are more likely to be willing to engage the intensity of Scorpio's feelings. Your steadiness is tested by Scorpio, yet his or her strong magnetism will entice you to hold on to the dream of "forever" with great hope and fortitude.

TAURUS–SAGITTARIUS (NOV. 22–DEC. 21)

You are going to have to make a number of
adjustments for this relationship to work. Gener-
ally, you tend to move slower than goal-oriented
Sagittarius. Your no-nonsense personality can offer
your Sagittarian lover a potential for stability and
focus regarding the practical side of life. On the
other hand, you can seem like a party spoiler as
you try to simplify your adventurous partner's life.
Under your steadfast influence, the restless archer
will either settle down or soon be tempted to point
his or her arrow in the direction of bigger dreams
and greener pastures. You may lack understanding
or acceptance of your partner's search for greater
horizons and unknown vistas. You'd rather create a
solid life built upon real pleasure and security. If,
however, you have Venus or Mercury in Aries, you
will be better equipped to accompany your lover in
whatever adventures he or she dreams up. But if
you have the Moon or Mars in Virgo or Pisces,
there may be stressful differences that are tough to
overcome. No matter what planetary pressures are
placed upon you as a couple, with some flexibility
you'll be able to dance and dream as you pave a
real road toward a rich and adventuresome life.

TAURUS–CAPRICORN (DEC. 22–JAN. 19)

These two earth signs are very compatible and tend to complement the virtues of stability, hard work, and patience within each other. Yet there are significant differences. You love the lush, green earth while the Capricorn may be drawn toward deserts and canyons. In other words, you may exhibit more emotions than cautious Capricorn. Trouble may arise as your partner tries to take the role of authoritarian. You may go along with this to a point, as long as you get your way on important matters of the heart. You'll trust your partner when it comes to making decisions about practical matters, but you won't want them to pick out home furnishings. You want things that indulge your senses, while Goats may be more practical in their needs. You can easily admire and deeply love your Capricorn, but problems can arise if your Venus is in Aries or Gemini, as your values may be quite different. Also, if your Moon is in Aries or Libra, compatibility may be more elusive. Success is likely within the format of a well-defined relationship where everything is spelled out. This partnership can achieve stability in the real world and can bring a heightened sense of ambition into your life.

TAURUS–AQUARIUS [JAN. 20–FEB. 18]

Your conventional ways are going to be tested by the radical and inventive antics of your Aquarian friend. You prefer physical comfort and don't like your senses rattled by uncertainty. Unfortunately, you may be jolted and surprised by the eccentric ways of Aquarius. You can be a soothing influence on your partner, for your earth can ground out the airy Aquarius. You're each more set in your ways than is at first apparent, as you're both fixed signs. When conflicts arise, your stubbornness is matched by your lover's unusual tactics—including the often difficult-to-accept realization that he or she knows everything. Let's face it: Aquarius is prone to mental arrogance, a trait intolerable to your down-to-earth approach. Another problem is that in your Aquarian's eyes, you are apt to become lazy and self-indulgent—character flaws he or she just will not succumb to. Yet other planetary placements can change the compatibility picture quite dramatically, making this combination outlast all the others. If the Moon or Mars in your chart is in any air sign, compatibility is enhanced. Loving kindness, tolerance, and understanding go a long way toward making this relationship a success.

TAURUS-PISCES (FEB. 19–MARCH 20)

Your earthy and practical character provides a supportive foundation for dreamy, watery Pisces, who thrives in a private world of nonverbal symbols and active imagination. Pisceans are empathetic and highly compassionate. Your down-to-earth sensibility mixes remarkably well with the Fish's refined attitudes toward love and relationships. Your planet is Venus. Pisces is associated with Neptune. Venus and Neptune play well together, especially when their physical senses meet up with fantasy. Your pursuit of love, whether through art, music, or people, is of the utmost importance to your Piscean partner. He or she knows how to pluck gently at your heart strings, melting away your stubbornness and making for a harmonic union. This is a good match, but other planetary placements in each chart can add complex dimensions to this relationship. If Mercury or Venus in your chart is in Aries, you may find it difficult to get along with your Pisces lover. On the other hand, if your Moon is in any water sign, compatibility is improved. You will need to give your Pisces mate enough encouragement and support so they don't feel too fragile around your solid determination.

ABOUT THE AUTHORS

RICK LEVINE When I first encountered astrology as a psychology undergraduate in the late 1960s, I became fascinated with the varieties of human experience. Even now, I love the one-on-one work of seeing clients and looking at their lives through the cosmic lens. But I also love history and utilize astrology to better understand the longer-term cycles of cultural change. My recent DVD, *Quantum Astrology*, explores some of these transpersonal interests. As a scientist, I'm always looking for patterns in order to improve my ability to predict the outcome of any experiment; as an artist, I'm entranced by the mystery of what we do not and cannot know. As an astrologer, I am privileged to live in an enchanted world that links the rational and magical, physical and spiritual—and yes—even science and art.

JEFF JAWER I'm a Taurus with a Scorpio Moon and Aries rising who lives in the Pacific Northwest with Danick, my double-Pisces wife, our two very well-behaved teenage Leo daughters, and two black Gemini cats (who are not so well-behaved). I have been a professional astrologer since 1973. I encountered astrology as my first marriage was ending. I was searching and needed to understand myself better. Astrology filled the bill. More than thirty years later, it remains the creative passion of my life as I continue to counsel, write, study, and share ideas with clients and colleagues around the world.

ACKNOWLEDGMENTS

Thanks to Paul O'Brien, our agent, our friend, and the creative genius behind Tarot.com; Gail Goldberg, the editor who always makes us sound better; Marcus Leaver and Michael Fragnito at Sterling Publishing, for their tireless support for the project; Barbara Berger, our supervising editor, who has shepherded this book with Taurean persistence and Aquarian invention; Laura Jorstad, for her refinement of the text; and Sterling project editor Mary Hern and designer Rachel Maloney for their invaluable help. We thank Bob Wietrak and Jules Herbert at Barnes & Noble, and all of the helping hands at Sterling. Thanks for the art and ideas from Jessica Abel and the rest of the Tarot.com team. Thanks as well to 3+Co. for the original design and to Tara Gimmer for the author photo.